Storymaking and Organizational Transformation

In a world undergoing continuous change, organizations find themselves facing the challenge of how to keep innovating to stay competitive. Inside any organization, people are the cornerstone on which innovation rests and builds, yet it is ever more difficult to engage everyone in designing their organization. This book explores and discusses how employees can be engaged digitally to assist innovation initiatives and lead to organizational transformation.

Storymaking and Organizational Transformation is based on the research activities of the platform IDeaLs during the year 2020 and provides a perspective on how employees can be helped to understand and even contribute to organizational innovation spontaneously. The book contributes to advancing understanding of engagement from two main perspectives: first, the authors introduce an approach based on storymaking; second, six cases are studied in depth and the application of the digital storymaking approach is explained. The authors introduce new ways of organizing in a context of ongoing change, as they bring forth the idea that engagement is a continuous practice of designing meaningful narratives which connect people and evolve along with them.

The book will appeal to both academics and practitioners across management fields. Scholars of innovation management and organization sciences will benefit from the extensive review of organizational transformation and innovation from a sensemaking perspective, whilst the practical, case studies provide a valuable resource for practitioners looking to effect change and manage transformation.

Tommaso Buganza is a Full Professor of Leadership and Innovation at the School of Management of Politecnico di Milano where he also is co-founder of LEADIN'Lab, the Laboratory for Leadership, Design, and Innovation. He is a lecturer in Innovation Management and Project Management, responsible for the Project Management Academy and coordinator of the innovation and training area at MIP (Politecnico di Milano Graduate School of Business). He is the scientific director of IDeaLs the global research platform of Politecnico di Milano that pioneers new ways to engage people to make innovation happen with companies. He co-founded Symplatform, the symposium on digital platforms that aims to foster constructive discussions among scholars and practitioners. He is the chairman of the scientific committee of the International Product Development Management Conference EIASM-IPDMC. His research activity explores the intersection between technological innovation and leadership and has been published in peer-reviewed journals.

Paola Bellis is an Assistant Professor at the School of Management of Politecnico di Milano and serves as director of IDeaLs, the global research platform that involves international companies pioneering new ways to engage people to make innovation happen. Her research interests are focused in the interplay between Innovation Management and Leadership. In particular, she has been working on the role of a team of dyads for the development of innovation in established companies, moreover she focuses on engagement strategies for innovation development.

Silvia Magnanini is a Post-Doc Researcher at the School of Management of Politecnico di Milano, where she serves as a researcher of LEADIN'Lab, the Laboratory for Leadership, Design, and Innovation. Her research interests are focused in Innovation and Design Management. She serves as a senior researcher in IDeaLs the global research platform of Politecnico di Milano that pioneers new ways to engage people to make innovation happen with companies. In particular, she has been researching about new collaborative practices to let employees converge toward an innovative vision.

Joseph Press is an Adjunct Professor of Strategic Design at the Parsons School of Design and a Visiting Professor at Politecnico di Milano Schools of Management and Design. He is also a Futures Advisor at the Institute For The Future where he advises organizations in the design of meaningful futures. After a 10-year career as an architect, including completing his PhD in Design Technology at MIT, he pivoted into management consulting. He capped his 15-year career at Deloitte by founding Deloitte Digital Switzerland, an interdisciplinary team focusing on the design of innovative digital experiences for global organizations across industries. He then became the Global Innovator at the Center for Creative Leadership, where he led leadership programs to co-create solutions to challenges requiring systemic transformation. To explore the intersections of his experiences in innovation, design, and leadership, he co-founded IDeaLs with the Leadin'Lab at the Politecnico di Milano.

Abraham B. (Rami) Shani is a Professor of Management at the Orfalea College of Business, California Polytechnic State University. His research interest includes collaborative research methodologies, work and organization design, organizational change and development, learning in and by organizations, sustainability, and sustainable effectiveness. His work was published in the *Academy of Management Journal*, *British Journal of Management*, *California Management Review*, *Human Relations*, *Journal of Applied Behavioral Science*, *Journal of Change Management*, *Organizational Dynamics*, *Sloan Management Review*, and others. His most recent book (co-authored with David Coghlan) is *Conducting Action Research* (SAGE, 2018). Since 2008 he is the co-editor of the annual research series, *Research in Organization Change and Development* (Emerald Publications). He served as the Management Department Head and Associate Dean at CalPoly and as the president of the Organization Development and Change Division at the Academy of Management. He is on the editorial board of five journals.

Daniel Trabucchi is an Assistant Professor at the School of Management, Politecnico di Milano, where he is part of LEADIN'Lab, the Laboratory for LEAdership, Design, and INnovation. He works on Innovation Management, with two main areas of research and teaching: platform-based business models and the human side of innovation (with strong focus on engagement and agile methods to make innovation happen, within the research platform IDeaLs). He is the scientific director of IDeaLs and he co-founded Symplatform, the symposium on digital platforms that aims to foster constructive discussions among scholars and practitioners.

His research has been published in peer-reviewed journals such as *Journal of Product Innovation Management*, *Technological Forecasting and Social Change*, *Internet Research*, *Research-Technology Management*, *Creativity and Innovation Management*, *Technology Analysis and*

Strategic Management, and *European Journal of Innovation Management*; he is also a reviewer for many of these journals.

Roberto Verganti is a Professor of Leadership and Innovation at the Stockholm School of Economics and Faculty of Design Theory and Practice at the Harvard Business School. He is also the founder of Leadin'Lab, the laboratory on the LEAdership, Design and INnovation of Politecnico di Milano, and scientific director of IDeaLs. Roberto has been a visiting scholar at the Copenhagen Business School and at the California Polytechnic State University and is an ambassador of the European Innovation Council of the European Commission. Roberto is the author of "*Overcrowded*", published by MIT Press in 2017 and of "*Design-Driven Innovation*", published by Harvard Business Press in 2009, which has been nominated by the Academy of Management for the George R. Terry Book Award as one of the best six management books published in 2008 and 2009. Roberto has issued more than 150 articles. He is in the Hall of Fame of the *Journal of Product Innovation Management* and has been featured on *The Wall Street Journal*, *The New York Times*, *Financial Times*, *Forbes*, and *BusinessWeek*. Roberto is a regular contributor to the *Harvard Business Review*.

Federico Paolo Zasa is a Post-Doc Researcher at the School of Management of Politecnico di Milano. He is a researcher of LEADIN'Lab, the Laboratory for LEAdership, Design, and Innovation, and also part of IDeaLs – Innovation and Design as Leadership, a research platform that investigates how to engage people to make innovation happen, where he focuses on the development of analytical tools for visual and text data. His research focuses on the cognitive aspects of the innovation process. In particular, he analyses how the interplay of cognitive diverse individuals and the establishment of a shared vision drive innovation.

Storymaking and Organizational Transformation

How the Co-creation of Narratives Engages People for Innovation and Transformation

Tommaso Buganza, Paola Bellis, Silvia Magnanini, Joseph Press, Abraham B. (Rami) Shani, Daniel Trabucchi, Roberto Verganti, and Federico Paolo Zasa

Routledge
Taylor & Francis Group
LONDON AND NEW YORK

First published 2023
by Routledge
4 Park Square, Milton Park, Abingdon, Oxon OX14 4RN

and by Routledge
605 Third Avenue, New York, NY 10158

Routledge is an imprint of the Taylor & Francis Group, an informa business

British Library Cataloguing-in-Publication Data
A catalogue record for this book is available from the British Library

ISBN: 978-1-032-23197-6 (hbk)
ISBN: 978-1-032-23198-3 (pbk)
ISBN: 978-1-003-27621-0 (ebk)

DOI: 10.4324/9781003276210

Typeset in Times New Roman
by codeMantra

Contents

Acknowledgments

The authors would like to thank all the partners of IDeaLs, without whom this book would never have seen the light.

In particular, we would like to thank **Nestlé** (in the persons of Joern Bruecker and Josefin Wahlberg), **Philips** (in the persons of Paul Gardien, Geert Christiaansen, and Clara Correia Martins), **Sasol** (in the persons of Billy Graham, Janita Naidoo, and Katharina Hanush), **Sintetica** (in the persons of Augusto Mitidieri and Davide Ferrara), **Sorgenia** (in the persons of Alberto Bigi, Thomas Greco, and Silvia Guidi), **STEF** (in the persons of Enrico Scotti, Fabio Cipolla, and Flavio d'Innocente)

A special thanks also goes to all the people from the partner companies who participated in the Story Making Experience, without their curiosity and active participation we would never have been able to learn all that we report in this book. A special thanks goes to Martina BARRI that shared with us part of this journey and played a relevant world in the data-gathering phase of this research.

The authors would like to thank the IDeaLs Brain Trust (Don Norman, Eun (Kim) Young, Gerhard Vorster) for your thoughtful feedback and participation to the platform development.

1 Introduction

1 The human side of innovation

Change is difficult. As human beings, we like our comfort zone and the safety of our old habits. Some of you might disagree. We are not all the same. Some feel the fire of innovation burning inside them, some like to think outside the box and continuously come up with new ideas. Nevertheless, we all – even those who feel the fire burning – agree that change is tiresome.

Let us take some examples from different fields to better understand. 2020 began with a totally unexpected event. Covid-19 pandemic stopped the world for months and has changed it significantly, maybe forever, in many respects. The pandemic provides us with at least two examples showing that change is actually a huge challenge.

The first one concerns teaching. If you were a student back in those months, if you had kids attending school, or if you simply heard the news talking about the challenges of remote teaching, you probably clearly understand the situation we are referring to. Literally from one day to the next, something considered only likely to happen in a Black Mirror episode (the TV series, lately produced by Netflix, that proposes dystopic futures starting from technology) became true. Millions of people started studying and attending lectures in front of a computer.

All the authors of this book teach. We teach in universities, we teach in corporations, and in many other situations. We had before us the technologies to do what we have done – and are still doing in some cases – since March 2020. But we had never done it before. Some of us had already been teaching remotely for some years in specific and flexible programs for executives. Still, it was different. It was a choice, a choice that the students made for a "different" experience. We felt that we were not entirely able to do everything we could in a physical

DOI: 10.4324/9781003276210-1

class. We set up breakout rooms for teamwork and we used shared screens and PowerPoint slides to "work together". Still, it was peculiar to that setting. Something chosen, somehow limiting, because "you cannot see the faces in front of you", because "people don't interact continuously, unless they have doubts", and so forth.

Then, something suddenly changed. We had to move all our programs online. All of them. Even for those who had not chosen to study remotely. Even those lectures that last four hours, or even six or eight hours per day. Even those where people have to work together. Even those where everyone must interact, talk, and contribute.

We were scared. Still, it happened. We did it. We leveraged the power of technologies that were already there before us and we were only partially using them. We discovered the magic world of collaborative tools like Miro and Mural that actually enabled all the research you'll be reading in this volume… because everything was designed before March 2020, using physical tools, but actually took place in those later months. We discovered that tools like Microsoft Teams, Zoom, amongst many others, had functions we had never seen, because we had not needed them, at least as much. We discovered that an Excel file with a list of links for breakout rooms was actually working, even when the software was (still) not supporting them. We discovered that we needed just two things. First, the time to understand the world we were entering, the software, and the norms of the digital world. Second, we needed to train people to join this new world along with us. Spending some minutes at the beginning of the class to set the stage, to explain what was acceptable and desirable (like turning on the camera, or just opening the mic and talking) and what was not (like keeping the mic on the entire session). And then a few more minutes to explain the basic tools that – guess what – were easy enough that everyone manage to use them.

All of that had already been possible for years. Still, we were not seeing enough reasons to go there. We were scared by the differences in our "normal" world. We had the chance to foster innovation for years, but we were not embracing it.

Some of you may think this is not innovation, this is not a desirable change, and that this was a way of dealing with an emergency. This is partly true, we discovered all of this through an emergency. But nevertheless, this is innovation. This is something that will stay with us. It will change, it will evolve, but it won't disappear. We still have many companies asking us to teach remotely, even if they could come to our campuses. This is cheaper. This is more inclusive. We can have people from all over the world in the same virtual room, enabling a corporate course even for those companies that have people spread around the globe that would otherwise not have been able to join a one-day course in another country. This is a more flexible way, in line with our professional and personal lives. We even discovered that – for some lectures – the pure digital setting is even better than the traditional one.

It was already there, but we were reluctant to embrace it because it was different from the status quo. Because it required us to change, as professionals, but also as human beings, challenging some of our beliefs.

The first point: aren't there less painful ways than an emergency to decide to foster innovation? This is what we'll propose in this volume.

This is just one of the many things that the pandemic has led us to understand. The second example we want to highlight is what happened over those months in March 2020 while the world was staying at home. Many, including ourselves, wondered what the future world would look like. We read articles imagining a world where the tracing apps for Covid-19 were just the starting point of a real and pervasive open data movement. It didn't happen. In many countries, those apps were a total disaster, with a very low percentage of people downloading and using them. Still, we have seen pictures of the new cities. Cities where anyone can cycle to avoid the crowded spaces of trains or subways. More sustainable cities where we understood that our consumption of resources is neither sustainable nor strictly necessary.

Yet, we are still stuck in traffic in our cars or on crowded trains to go to work. Not all of us, but certainly the vast majority.

The second point: even an emergency may not be enough, how can we set transformation in motion? How can we help people in making innovation happen?

Imagining a new world may not be the easiest thing, but it is definitely easier than making it happen.

It is not enough to see the new desired direction to actually change. People need to transform themselves. To see things differently, to make them their own, and then enact new behaviors. This is what happened with remote teaching. Having no choice, we embraced the tools and technologies that were already there in front of us. And we changed our behaviors. We started seeing things differently, we are different.

This is what this book is about. This book is not about envisioning innovation, this book is about transforming people to make innovation happen.

2 Innovation and change management: a painful journey?

When we refer to innovation in a broader sense than product or process innovation, we cross over to the world of change management.

In organizational innovation, strategic innovation, or even business model innovation, we deal with aspects that necessarily require people within the organizational boundaries to behave differently in the "new world". This is where change management comes in. Change management refers to all the approaches that prepare and support individuals, teams, and the overall organization to achieve organizational transformation.

We looked into change management theories and models and want to briefly talk about two that grabbed our attention the most. These models that we use in teaching change management are extremely valuable, but have an underlying assumption that we would like to dispel.

The first works at the individual level and is used to explain individuals' reactions to change, going through a series of phases. It is the five stages of grief or the Kübler–Ross model. It postulates that those experiencing grief go through a series of five emotions: denial, anger, bargaining, depression, and acceptance. It is a very popular model, even if criticized for its imprecision. Originally developed for people dealing with a terminal illness, over the years, it expanded to personal loss, the end of a relationship, the loss of a job, and ultimately achieved prominence also in organizational change management literature (Scire, 2007).

The second is the burning platform model. In 1993, Daryl Conner introduced this metaphor in his book "*Managing at the speed of change*" to describe high-level urgency change initiatives. What does it mean? Have you ever found yourself facing a new information system in your organization that you did not want to use? If at a certain point, the old one were to close down, you would definitely have to jump into the new one. This is the approach deriving from the burning platform idea. You cannot avoid changing, the old place is burning, and you can no longer stay there. This does not differ greatly from what we described with our digital teaching experience during the pandemic, and well, there was an actual burning platform.

The typical steps of devising a burning platform enable building a narrative that explores the need for change, linking it back to customers or to something more valuable, and then bringing people onboard and managing resistance.

The two models are useful, even effective most of the time. Still, they have an underlying assumption: change is bad. It is like a disease. Or even worse, to make it happen you need to set fire to the old place. Is this actually necessary?

Traditional change management theories posit that people are unwilling to change when innovation is introduced. We find this statement not to be true: people want to innovate, to the extent that they find meaning in what they do (Verganti, 2009, 2017). Still, what we see is that it is difficult for people to embrace change and start enacting new behaviors. This book is about helping people embrace change through new behaviors, building something positive that does not concern illness or burning places.

3 Introducing storymaking as a way to transform people

This volume is about our research journey to understand how to transform people to make innovation happen. It is the work of a group of researchers and companies that – within the IDeaLs project (described at the end of the book if you wish to know more) – experiments with new ways to foster innovation.

Our approach is built on what emerged in the two previous sections. First, we are interested in generating real change, not just ideas for change. Second, we want to build on human energy and the positive side of innovation, leaving aside any negative metaphors of innovation as a scaring, intimidating yet inevitable problem to an opportunity of growth and prosperity. Indeed, we believe in three pillars:

- Innovation as meaning: we believe that people embrace innovation if they find their own meaning in it, in other words, if the innovation is meaningful to them as human beings.
- Design as engagement: we believe that people need to design the change to feel it, in other words, everyone needs to be engaged in the process.
- Leadership as a community: we believe that leadership is a collective act, in other words, change cannot happen alone, people need others to reflect and act with.

Building on these three principles, we developed a collaborative research project with more than 70 workshops over the course of a year with six partner companies that worked with us with a clear objective: experimenting with how to transform people to make innovation happen.

This introductory chapter reflects the premise upon which we built our research orientation. We told you a story. The story of teaching and exploring in the era of a global pandemic. We brought you into our world to engage you in reading this book, to share our collective discovery journey, and to generate interest in what we have done and what we'll be doing over the next chapters.

This is the power of storytelling, it helps people imagine a world, it engages people in it, it shows people why it is interesting, why it is relevant, and how to trigger impact. Indeed, storytelling is one of the most used and diffused tools to help people embrace change in organizations. Nevertheless, it lacks some of the elements we have mentioned here. It tends to be top-down, it does not leave much space for your particular meaning. It does not give you space to co-create. It does not involve others to create shared meaning and understanding. And more importantly, it is not necessarily directly link to action. And what we learned from the story at the beginning of the chapter is that for innovation to happen, we must enact actual behaviors. Therefore, this book won't be talking about storytelling. It will talk about *storymaking* and the collaborative approach we developed to help organizations foster new behaviors.

Chapter 2 digs deeper into this reflection, bringing you into the world of stories and their use in the management world, defining our view of storymaking. Chapter 3 describes what we have actually done, our collaborative research approach, and the methods we applied. In particular, this chapter introduces the platform dimension of our research programs. To provide a broader view of the transformation process to make innovation happen, we also explore three specific dimensions that emerged as critical from the collaboration: intimacy in innovation, convergence in innovation, and the cognitive dimension of transformation. Chapter 4 tells the stories of the organizations that took part in this journey and enabled us to discover much more in the world of innovation. Chapter 5 explores the results in relation to the three dimensions (intimacy, convergence, and cognition) explored in the stories. Finally, Chapter 6 presents some concluding remarks. Welcome on board, we hope you'll enjoy this journey into the world of storymaking to make innovation happen.

References

Conner, D. (1993). *Managing at the speed of change: How resilient managers succeed and prosper where others fail.* New York: Random House.

Scire, P. (2007). *Applying grief stages to organizational change. An attributional analysis of the Kübler-Ross model of dying.* Cambridge, MA: Harvard University.

Verganti, R. (2009). *Design driven innovation: Changing the rules of competition by radically innovating what things mean.* Boston, MA: Harvard Business Press.

Verganti, R. (2017). *Overcrowded: Designing meaningful products in a world awash with ideas.* Cambridge, MA: MIT Press.

2 The Role of Stories in Management

1 Stories and Management

We live in a world completely overwhelmed with ideas and opportunities (Verganti, 2017). Digital technologies enhance organizational capabilities to innovate (Verganti et al., 2020; Press et al., 2021), but innovation requires change. To keep pace with novel scenarios, organizations have to transform (García-Morales et al., 2006), and engaging people in these transformations is crucial for innovation to happen (Edmondson, 2012, 2019).

Innovation is not the mere act of developing products, but requires organizational engagement (Zaltman et al., 1973; Lee et al., 2012; Garcia Martinez, 2015) that will allow people to make sense and become familiar with the new scenario, shaping their identities in relation to the change (Humphreys & Brown, 2002; Cunliffe & Coupland, 2012). Indeed, innovation is a sensemaking process whereby people shape new identities, both individual and collective (Weick et al., 2005). This collective sensemaking is the result of a continuous process of rewriting the organizational narrative: everyone is at the same time the narrator and listener involved in formulating, editing, or refuting elements of the new story (Humphreys & Brown, 2002).

It is widely acknowledged that stories have for thousands of years shaped the way we live, as evidenced by the dramatic discovery of cave paintings from 30,000 years ago in Chauvet and Lascaux in France. The lives of our ancestors depended on narratives through which tales and lessons from the past were transmitted from one generation to the next. As well as a form of collective memory, stories were used to deal with complex social situations, a tool to stimulate imagination and develop empathy toward fictional contexts and people. Most ancient stories, such as the Epic of Gilgamesh or Homer's Odyssey, strived to make humans identify with the lives of kings or heroes struggling with social

DOI: 10.4324/9781003276210–2

dilemmas or moral decisions (Boyd, 2010). Through Gilgamesh, audiences experienced the trade-off between the expression of unlimited power and respect for others, through Odyssey, his struggle between immortality and Calypso, and the desire to return to Penelope in Ithaca.

Much of what we know of societies preceding ours stems from tales or written documents narrating the past. How we interpret these stories shape our individual and social identities. The United States was the scene of the American Civil Rights movement when actress Nichelle Nichols experienced the indissoluble link between stories and people's lives. Nichelle was considering leaving the popular TV series Star Trek in which she stunned the general public as one of the first black women cast as the main character in a major television show. But it was Martin Luther King himself who encouraged her to remain in her role as a symbol of a brighter world with a more progressive social system. Inspired by real-life experiences, stories overlap with reality and create new ways of understanding the world around us and our role in society (Zaidi, 2019).

Even today, we play as children through stories and love to hear tales from our parents. Growing up, we continue our encounters with stories in books, films, or theatre shows. It is in the nature of human beings to think narratively rather than argumentatively or paradigmatically (Weick, 1995). By thinking in narratives, we make sense of the world around us (Maitlis & Christianson, 2014). Stories enable sequential reasoning through which we make sense of events. They help in dealing with the unacceptable, making it manageable for the individual. Stories evoke a mix of curiosity and fear, the pretext for understanding and action (Weick, 1995; Humphreys & Brown, 2002; Cunliffe & Coupland, 2012). Stories bring coherence and allow us to make sense of a chaotic and illogical world (Steuer & Wood, 2008).

2 How stories shape organizational routines

In recent years, stories and narratives have gained momentum as a means of communication (Gabriel, 2000; Enninga & van der Lugt, 2016) even in the field of the organization (Boje, 2008; Denning, 2010; Czarniawska, 2013), facilitating understanding complex processes (Browning & Boudès, 2005; Kurtz & Snowden, 2007; Brown, 2009), but also contributing to problem-solving and decision-making (Brown & Duguid, 1991). Organizations leverage storytelling as an instrument for two main purposes: to smoothen the development of innovation projects (Enninga & van der Lugt, 2016), and to manage broader transformation and change (Weinpress et al., 2018).

In innovation projects, storytelling is an effective communication and knowledge management tool (Brusamolin & Moresi, 2008; Czarniawska, 2013; Sankaran, 2018). First, narratives serve as translation devices across boundaries (Bartel & Garud, 2009; Enninga & van der Lugt, 2016) and have a strategic role in dealing with multiple stakeholders (Vaagaasar, 2011). Second, stories facilitate sensemaking, thus a valuable tool to create new constructs (Tsoukas & Hatch, 2001; Czarniawska, 2005). This highlights the participatory nature of storytelling where the intersection of multiple voices leads to the emergence of a collective narrative (Tsoukas & Hatch, 2013). In this sense, a recent line of research has focused on the systemic nature of collective storytelling (Bushe & Marshak, 2015; Saltmarshe, 2018; Talgorn & Hendriks, 2021; Talgorn et al., 2022) where integrating a set of parallel stories results in a system that triggers multiple levels of comprehension, analysis, and action. Despite the many examples in classical literature of this fictional ploy – such as Italo Calvino's *If on a Winter's Night a Traveller* or Philip Roth's *The Counterlife* – this practice has not yet reached its full potential in the organizational context.

In the context of large-scale transformations, stories are mainly used to engage and onboard people for specific business purposes (Klein, 2005; Denning, 2006, 2008). Stories enable people to make sense of change (Reissner, 2011). Storytelling has proven a powerful way to present a novel scenario and draw valuable outcomes from inferences within the narrative (Kleiner & Roth, 1997; Roth & Kleiner, 1998; Snowden, 2000). Indeed, in the organizational context, individuals often perceive change as a threat: the need to adopt new norms and behaviors causes discomfort (Steuer & Wood, 2008). Hence, when innovation is introduced, individuals might feel lost and experience a lack of meaning. In this sense, narratives represent a "safe space" where ideas can flourish and knowledge can be exchanged (Buckler & Zien, 1996). Stories facilitate a new sense of self-perception, as they allow the shaping of new meanings: they provide an intimate experience that enables individuals to make sense and become familiar with the new organizational space (Cunliffe & Coupland, 2012).

3 Achieving change through storytelling

To engage people, effective narratives must be plausible and rational (Denning, 2006; Cunliffe & Coupland, 2012), even if the appropriate approach to identify an engaging story is still under discussion (Denning, 2006). Denning (2006) argues that each narrative must be tailored to the specific business purpose, e.g., to spark action, transmit values, foster collaboration, or share knowledge. As an example, springboard stories should be told in a minimalist fashion to enable listeners to participate in imagining the stories. This differs from future-oriented leadership stories, as it is difficult to craft a rational narrative about a future that is unknown (Denning, 2006; Hill et al., 2014).

The management literature often assumes that organizational change requires managing internal resistance, and the role of stories is to depict an ideal outcome. Thus, in the organizational field, storytelling plays an important role in organization' strategy, development, and learning processes (Boje, 2008) and is mainly used as a top-down tool to communicate and convince (Klein, 2005; Denning, 2006; Weinpress et al., 2018). But organizational sensemaking is a collective endeavor that requires individuals to assimilate and reframe external cues, in turn requiring a perspective of active involvement (Weick, 1995; Cunliffe & Coupland, 2006; Stigliani & Ravasi, 2012).

4 Design practices in organizations

A significant body of research has investigated how designerly practices enable sensemaking through co-creation (Brown, 2009; Dell'Era et al., 2020). Practices such as design thinking are gaining momentum in the management field, as they spark commitment across the whole organization (Holloway, 2009; Martin, 2017).

Originating in studies on the creative process, the design-based practices of manipulating signs and text are key to transferring, transforming, and materializing knowledge across different boundaries of the organization (Carlile, 2002; Kolko, 2010; Zurlo & Cautela, 2014; Calabretta et al., 2016). Artifacts, such as prototypes or visual representations, allow people to make innovation tangible (Holloway, 2009; DeLarge, 2010). Design tools, such as personas and storyboards, might be applied in a descriptive approach to illustrate new products or services (Brown, 2009; Liedtka, 2014; Dell'Era et al., 2020). Scenarios, vignettes, and other representation tools might take a prospective approach to design new strategic visions and future desired outcomes (Rhisiart, 2013; Brassett & O'Reilly, 2015; Manzini, 2015; Verganti, 2017).

Among these artifacts, a significant number of studies recognize stories as an instrument to promote collective sensemaking for innovation (Brown, 2009; DeLarge, 2010; Stigliani & Ravasi, 2012; Dell'Era et al., 2020). Narratives are conceived as "powerful mechanisms for translating ideas across the organization so that they are comprehensible"

(Bartel & Garud, 2009), sustaining social interactions throughout the design process (Lloyd, 2000; Rill, 2016).

In particular, storytelling introduces a narrative element in the designing activity: encoding social experiences and linking diverse viewpoints and actions over time (Lloyd, 2000; Boje, 2008; Rhisiart, 2013; Rill, 2016; Press et al., 2021). Stories help in framing ambiguity or paradoxical situations by visualizing possibilities (Zurlo & Cautela, 2014). Narratives remain sufficiently open so that the story's reader or listener is required to fill gaps through imagination (Price et al., 2018). Nevertheless, scholars acknowledge that the ways of implementing stories in organizations are still under scrutiny (Gill, 2011). Indeed, the process of collaboratively shaping an artifact is more valuable than the artifact itself (Schön, 1983; Tversky, 2014; Calabretta et al., 2016). The design dialogue behind the co-creation activity contains a wealth of information on meaning-exchange among stakeholders, while the interweaving of different narratives helps create a shared understanding and sense of collective ownership (Sanders & Stappers, 2008; Stigliani & Ravasi, 2012; Rill, 2016; Press et al., 2021). Creative narratives convey tacit knowledge, values, and beliefs, thus shaping the identity of individuals and enhancing their behavior (Rhodes & Brown, 2005; Cagnin, 2018).

5 The designerly practice of storymaking

This storymaking approach leads individuals to update their frames and take coherent action (Weick, 1995; Enninga & van der Lugt, 2016). Recent studies show that the creation of narratives facilitates both divergent and convergent thinking, boosting the sensemaking process (Weick et al., 2005). The practice of storymaking facilitates innovation-oriented sensemaking, as individuals enact cues from the new environment and update their cognitive frames (Blomquist & Lundin, 2010; Enninga & van der Lugt, 2016). Table 2.1 captures the main differences between storytelling and storymaking. The present study aims to explore storymaking as a collective process sense making of a new scenario in an innovative environment (Enninga & van der Lugt, 2016): engaging people in making sense of a new vision by shaping their identities through the creation of personal stories. In particular, we aim to answer the following research question: *What is the effect of design-based engagement practices, such as storymaking, on continuous employee engagement over time?*

To provide an answer to our research question, we focus on designing a storytelling-based experience in which individuals write their

Table 2.1 Storytelling and storymaking: synopsis of a comparative perspective

	Storytelling	*Storymaking*
Organizational change	Organizational process to be managed (Weinpress et al., 2018)	Individual sense-perception process (Cunliffe & Coupland, 2012)
Purpose	Engagement toward an objective (Klein, 2005; Denning, 2008)	Update frames and guide action (Weick, 1995)
Function	Communication tool to convince (Denning, 2006; Denning, 2008)	Discursive tool to create (Maitlis & Christianson, 2014)
Main applications	Knowledge management (Brusamolin & Moresi, 2008; Sankaran, 2018)	Design new meanings (Humphreys & Brown, 2002)
	Transmission of extrinsic business objectives (Denning, 2006)	Shaping intrinsic identities (Humphreys & Brown, 2002; Cunliffe & Coupland, 2012)
How stories are used	Monodirectional (Klein, 2005)	Bidirectional (Cunliffe & Coupland, 2012)
	Top-down (Denning, 2008)	Bottom-up and top-down (Cunliffe & Coupland, 2012)

own stories to make sense of innovation, and the sum of these individual changes then generates organizational transformation.

References

Bartel, C. A., & Garud, R. (2009). The role of narratives in sustaining organizational innovation. *Organization Science*, 20(1), 107–117.

Blomquist, T., & Lundin, R. A. (2010). Projects are real, virtual or what? *International Journal of Managing Projects in Business*, 3(1), 10–21.

Boje, D. M. (2008). *Storytelling organizations*. Thousand Oaks, CA: SAGE.

Boyd, B. (2010). *On the origin of stories: Evolution, cognition, and fiction*. Cambridge, MA: Harvard University Press.

Brassett, J., & O'Reilly, J. (2015). Styling the future. A philosophical approach to design and scenarios. *Futures*, 74, 37–48.

Brown, J. S., & Duguid, P. (1991). Organizational learning and communities-of-practice: Toward a unified view of working, learning, and innovation. *Organization Science*, 2(1), 40–57.

Brown, T. (2009). *Change by design: How design thinking transforms organizations and inspires innovation*. New York: HarperCollins.

Browning, L., & Boudès, T. (2005). The use of narrative to understand and respond to complexity: A comparative analysis of the Cynefin and Weickian models. *E: Co*, 7(3–4), 32–39.

Brusamolin, V., & Moresi, E. (2008). Narrativas de histórias: Um estudo preliminar na gestão de projetos de tecnologia da informação. *Ciência Da Informação*, 37(1), 37–52.

Buckler, S. A., & Zien, K. A. (1996). The spirituality of innovation: Learning from stories. *Journal of Product Innovation Management: An International Publication of the Product Development & Management Association*, 13(5), 391–405.

Cagnin, C. (2018). Developing a transformative business strategy through the combination of design thinking and futures literacy. *Technology Analysis & Strategic Management*, 30(5), 524–539.

Calabretta, G., Gemser, G., & Karpen, I. (2016). *Strategic design: Eight essential practices every strategic designer must master.* Amsterdam: BIS Publishers.

Carlile, P. R. (2002). A pragmatic view of knowledge and boundaries: Boundary objects in new product development. *Organization Science*, 13, 442, 455–456.

Cunliffe, A., & Coupland, C. (2012). From hero to villain to hero: Making experience sensible through embodied narrative sensemaking. *Human Relations*, 65(1), 63–88.

Czarniawska, B. (2005). Karl Weick: Concepts, style and reflection. *The Sociological Review*, 53(1_suppl), 267–278.

Czarniawska, B. (2013). Storytelling: A managerial tool and its local translations. In Drori, G.S., Höllerer, M.A., & Walgenbach, P. (Eds.). *Global Themes and Local Variations in Organization and Management: Perspectives on Glocalization* (1st ed.) (pp. 81–94). London: Routledge. https://doi.org/10.4324/9780203139486

DeLarge, C. (2010). Storytelling as a critical success factor in design processes and outcomes. *Design Management Review*, 15(3), 76–81.

Dell'Era, C., Magistretti, S., Cautela, C., Verganti, R., & Zurlo, F. (2020). Four kinds of design thinking: From ideating to making, engaging, and criticizing. *Creativity and Innovation Management*, 29(2), 324–344. https://doi.org/10.1111/caim.12353

Denning, S. (2006). Effective storytelling: Strategic business narrative techniques. *Strategy & Leadership*, 34(1), 42–48.

Denning, S. (2008). How leaders can use powerful narratives as change catalysts. *Strategy & Leadership*, 36(2), 11–15.

Denning, S. (2010). A leader's guide to radical management of continuous innovation. *Strategy & Leadership*, 38(4), 11–16.

Edmondson, A. C. (2012). *Teaming: How organizations learn, innovate, and compete in the knowledge economy.* San Francisco, CA: Jossey-Bass.

Edmondson, A. C. (2019). *The fearless organization.* Hoboken, NJ: Wiley.

Enninga, T., & van der Lugt, R. (2016). The innovation journey and the skipper of the raft: About the role of narratives in innovation project leadership. *Project Management Journal*, 47(2), 103–114.

Gabriel, Y. (2000). *Storytelling in organizations: Facts, fictions, and fantasies.* Oxford: OUP.

Garcia Martinez, M. (2015). Solver engagement in knowledge sharing in crowdsourcing communities: Exploring the link to creativity. *Research Policy*, 44(8), 1419–1430.

García-Morales, V. J., Llorens-Montes, F. J., & Verdú-Jover, A. J. (2006). Antecedents and consequences of organizational innovation and organizational learning in entrepreneurship. *Industrial Management and Data Systems*, 106(1), 21–42.

Gill, R. (2011). Using storytelling to maintain employee loyalty during change. *International Journal of Business and Social Science*, 2(15), 23–32.

Hill, L. A., Brandeau, G., Truelove, E., & Lineback, K. (2014). *Collective genius: The art and practice of leading innovation.* Boston, MA: Harvard Business Review Press.

Holloway, M. (2009). How tangible is your strategy? How design thinking can turn your strategy into reality. *Journal of Business Strategy*, 30(2–3), 50–56. https://doi.org/10.1108/02756660910942463

Humphreys, M., & Brown, A. D. (2002). Narratives of organizational identity and identification: A case study of hegemony and resistance. *Organization Studies*, 23(3), 421–447.

Klein, L. (2005). Systemic inquiry exploring organisations. *Kybernetes*, 34 (3/4), 439–447.

Kleiner, A., & Roth, G. (1997). *Learning histories: A new tool for turning organizational experience into action.* New 21st Century Working Papers Series 002. Cambridge, MA: MIT Center for Coordination Science.

Kolko, J. (2010). Abductive thinking and sensemaking: The drivers of design synthesis. *Design Issues*, 26(1), 15–28. https://doi.org/10.1162/desi.2010.26.1.15

Kurtz, C. F., & Snowden, D. (2007). Bramble bushes in a thicket. Narrative and the intangibles of learning networks. In Gibbert, M. & Durand, T. (Eds.), *Strategic networks: Learning to compete* (pp. 121–150). Malden, MA: Blackwell Publishing.

Lee, S. M., Olson, D. L., & Trimi, S. (2012). Innovative collaboration for value creation. *Organizational Dynamics*, 41(1), 7–12.

Liedtka, J. (2014). Innovative ways companies are using design thinking. *Strategy & Leadership*, 42(2), 40–45.

Lloyd, P. (2000). Storytelling and the development of discourse in the engineering design process. *Design Studies*, 21(4), 357–373.

Maitlis, S., & Christianson, M. (2014). Sensemaking in organizations: Taking stock and moving forward. *Academy of Management Annals*. https://doi.org/10.1080/19416520.2014.873177

Manzini, E. (2015). *Design, when everybody design.* Cambridge, MA: MIT Press.

Martin, R. (2017). Use design thinking to build commitment to a new idea. *Harvard Business Review*, Published on HBR.COM January 3, 2017.

Press, J., Bellis, P., Buganza, T., Magnanini, S., Shani, A. B. (Rami), Trabucchi, D., Verganti, R., & Zasa, F. (2021). *IDeaLs: Transformation in the digital era*. Bingley: Emerald.

Price, R., Matthews, J., & Wrigley, C. (2018). Three narrative techniques for engagement and action in design-led innovation. *She Ji: The Journal of Design, Economics, and Innovation*, 4(2), 186–201. https://doi.org/10.1016/j.sheji.2018.04.001

Reissner, S. C. (2011). Patterns of stories of organisational change. *Journal of Organizational Change Management*, 24(5), 593–609.

Rhisiart, M. (2013). Exploring the future for arts and culture organisations through scenarios and vignettes. *Futures*, 50, 15–24.

Rhodes, C., & Brown, A. D. (2005b). Writing responsibly: narrative fiction and organization studies. *Organization*, 12, 467–491.

Rill, B. (2016). Resonant co-creation as an approach to strategic innovation. *Journal of Organizational Change Management*, 29(7), 1135–1152.

Roth, G., & Kleiner, A. (1998). Developing organizational memory through learning histories. *Organizational Dynamics*, 27(2), 43–60.

Saltmarshe, E. (2018). Using stories to change systems. *Stanford Social Innovation Review.* Available at https://ssir.org/articles/entry/using_story_to_change_systems#

Sanders, E. B., & Stappers, P. J. (2008). Co-creation and the new landscapes of design. *Codesign*, 4(1), 5–18.

Sankaran, S. (2018). Megaproject management and leadership: A narrative analysis of life stories' past and present. *International Journal of Managing Projects in Business*, 11, 53–79.

Schön, D. A. (1983). *The reflective practitioner: How professionals think in action*. London: Temple-Smith.

Snowden, D. (2000). Organic knowledge management: Part I the ASHEN model: An enabler of action. *Knowledge Management*, 3(7), 14–17.

Steuer, R., & Wood, T. (2008). Storytellers and their discursive strategies in a post-acquisition process. *Journal of Organizational Change Management*, 21(5), 574–588. https://doi.org/10.1108/09534810810903225

Stigliani, I., & Ravasi, D. (2012). Organizing thoughts and connecting brains: Material practices and the transition from individual to group-level prospective sensemaking. *Academy of Management Journal*, 55(5), 1232–1259.

Talgorn, E., Hendriks, M., Geurts, L., & Bakker, C. (2022). A Storytelling Methodology to Facilitate User-Centered Co-Ideation between Scientists and Designers. *Sustainability (Switzerland)*, 14(7), [4132]. https://doi.org/10.3390/su14074132

Tsoukas, H., & Hatch, M. J. (2013). Complex thinking, complex practice: The case for a narrative approach to organizational complexity. In MacIntosh, R., MacLean, D., Stacey, R., & Griffin, D. (Eds.), *Complexity and organization: Readings and conversations* (pp. 247–276). London: Routledge.

Tversky, B. (2014). The cognitive design of tools of thought. *Review of Philosophy and Psychology*, 6(1), 99–116.
Vaagaasar, A. L. (2011). Development of relationships and relationship competencies in complex projects. *International Journal of Managing Projects in Business*, 4(2), 294–307.
Verganti, R. (2017). *Overcrowded: Designing meaningful products in a world awash with ideas.* Cambridge, MA: MIT Press.
Verganti, R., Vendraminelli, L., & Iansiti, M. (2020). Innovation and design in the age of artificial intelligence. *Journal of Product Innovation Management*, 37(3), 212–227.
Weick, K. E. (1995). *Sensemaking in organizations (foundations for organizational science).* Thousand Oaks, CA: Sage Publications Inc.
Weick, K. E., Sutcliffe, K. M., & Obstfeld, D. (2005). Organizing and the process of sensemaking. *Organization Science*, 16(4), 409–421.
Weinpress, A., Bieler, A., Gelbetz, R. E., & Or, E. (2018). Branding an academic superbrand. *Journal of Brand Strategy*, 7(2), 117–140.
Zaidi, L. (n.d.). Worldbuilding in science fiction. *Foresight and Design*, 12.
Zaltman, G., Duncan, R., & Holbek, J. (1973). *Innovation and organizations.* New York: Wiley.
Zurlo, F., & Cautela, C. (2014). Design strategies in different narrative frames. *Design Issues*, 30(1), 19–35.

3 The Research Approach

1 Introduction

The management, innovation, and design fields are rapidly evolving, and so are the research methodologies to study the related phenomena. Our research adheres to Mode 2 knowledge production paradigm, adopting a hybrid methodology of action research and design science research. This is a collaborative approach in that the research question and research process are co-developed by the research team and practitioners. Specifically, the research and management teams converged on answering the question of how engagement in an organizational transformation project can be created and maintained. This process then led to the development of the storymaking approach, an evolution of the better-known storytelling method: we describe how we move from organizational stories to human stories, from human stories to personal stories, and from personal stories back again to organizational stories, then coalescing around an organization-wide storyworld.

We designed, developed, and tested this approach in collaboration with six partner organizations (Nestlè, Philips, Sasol, Sintetica, Sorgenia, and STEF). Storymaking consists of a series of workshops where individuals are supported by a card set to make sense of organizational transformation. Everyone designs their own transformation story, highlighting the direction and support needed. Critical reflection takes place in pairs and teams, and everyone commits to some specific concrete action. We then measure the engagement and the meaningfulness of the designed story.

This project is a research platform that contributes to research and practice: we study the role of intimacy in innovation, convergence in a shared direction, cognition, and transformation. Through action

DOI: 10.4324/9781003276210-3

research, we also support the sensemaking process of every participant *in situ*.

2 Research design and methodological approach

The management, design, and innovation research fields continue to evolve; as they mature, so do the different streams of thought and practices in terms of research orientation and methodologies. At a very basic level, all three are embedded in the concerns of members of a system, such as an organization, and tend to focus on generating actionable knowledge, often through collaborative inquiry.

Scholars have long debated the issues associated with the nature of knowledge and human knowing (Meynell, 1998). Disagreements and debates regarding different research processes, outcomes, and knowledge creation in general have moved the philosophical discourse over the centuries (Coghlan et al., 2019). One outcome of these debates and their intensity is the polarization between theory and practice, understanding and action, rigor and relevance – in other words, between the two knowledge production paradigms labeled Mode 1 and Mode 2.

Mode 1 and Mode 2 knowledge production labels, elaborating different research approaches, were introduced by Gibbons and his colleagues (Gibbons et al., 1994, 2011; Nowotny et al., 2001). Mode 1 is the type of knowledge created by universities or research centers following a traditional theoretical or experimental sciences approach. This type of academic knowledge is largely explanatory and driven by a research agenda to address an identifiable knowledge gap often linked to the evolution of a knowledge domain within a specific discipline. Usually, the type and content of the knowledge generated are firmly related to the field's evolution.

This is both a major advantage and drawback of Mode 1 paradigm. Knowledge is produced by building on a solid backbone of rigorous academic research methodology. Theoretical and empirical reflections aim to develop new theories and then test them, attempting to unveil the universal laws that govern the working principles of complex systems. Yet, the very nature of the field limits the usefulness, relevance, and impact of the results (MacIntosh et al., 2021; Mirvis et al., 2021). Oftentimes, the field evolves more rapidly than academic research, and even when one such universal law is discovered and tested, years are needed before the required evidence can be gathered so that the theory is considered valid (Coghlan et al., 2020).

As an example, consider the phenomenon of sensemaking. As discussed in the previous chapter, sensemaking is the process of gathering cues from the environment and translating them into concrete action. Certainly central to the idea of sensemaking in organizations is the knowledge that Weick (1995) developed starting from his seminal book *Sensemaking in Organizations*. Various scholars then continued developing this knowledge, including Stigliani and Ravasi's (2012) concept development study, and Lüscher and Lewis' (2008) analysis of managerial sensemaking. Published in the same journal, the two studies demonstrate a radically different approach to the study of sensemaking.

While Stigliani and Ravasi (2012) studied the design consultancy Continuum to unveil the patterns in organizational sensemaking, Lüscher and Lewis (2008) supported a change initiative at the Danish company Lego, and were actively involved in supporting the sensemaking process. The first study focuses on identifying a general pattern in how collaborative sensemaking takes place. The authors identify a four-stage process (noticing and bracketing, articulating, elaborating, and influencing) that a collective of individuals goes through when needing to make some sense of their environment. This process leads to an explanation of how concept development takes place and sheds light on the underlying principles. Once this general process has been identified, it should be easy for managers to understand which levers to activate to increase the performance of a specific dimension.

In line with Mode 1 knowledge production paradigm, Stigliani and Ravasi's (2012) main goal was to advance the academic discourse around the sensemaking process by unveiling the underlying patterns. Despite the explanatory nature of the study, it is often difficult to apply in a practical setting. The generalizations needed to bestow the findings validity are the same that limit its applicability in a specific context.

Mode 2 paradigm tackles this problem from the opposite side. Starting from a concrete organizational problem, Mode 2 researchers aim for theoretical development in a situated practice, namely working with the world of practice.

The study of Lüscher and Lewis (2008) exemplifies this second situation brilliantly. At the end of the 20th century, the then CEO Kjeld Kirk Kristiansen hired the executive Poul Plougmann to restructure the organization. The individuals who suffered most from this change were the middle management who needed to connect the strategic and operational levels in the organization and were caught between the hammer and the anvil (Lüscher & Lewis, 2008). Rather than merely studying the situation with the purpose of extracting globally valid principles, the authors adopted a radically different approach consisting of action research that lasted several months, actively supporting the middle management's sensemaking process. In this case, the actual production of knowledge was tightly bound to the context. The benefits of this study were twofold: it provided actionable insights to support the company undergoing change, and; the authors developed theoretical knowledge about scientific sensemaking.

Mode 2 consists of knowledge production with five main characteristics: (1) it is generated in the application context and seeks to address practical issues; (2) it is transdisciplinary, mobilizing a range of theoretical perspectives and practical methodologies to solve problems; (3) it is socially accountable and reflexive, sensitive to the research process itself and to the transdisciplinary dynamics; (4) it is heterogeneous in that participation is flexible and might change in line with specific project requirements; and (5) it requires forms of quality control grounded in the previous four characteristics pertaining to its practical orientation, transdisciplinarity, social accountability, and heterogeneity.

While Mode 1 and Mode 2 are grounded in distinct and often opposing philosophical principles, methods from Mode 1 may be used in Mode 2 in management and innovation research (Coghlan et al., 2020; Shani & Coghlan, 2021a). This research is rooted in Mode 2 paradigm, but as we will see also integrated Mode 1 methods to address research questions that emerged as the study progressed.

3 Collaborative research and Mode 2 paradigm

This project is a research platform that unites researchers and organizations seeking to develop meaningful and robust research to advance knowledge both from a theoretical and practical point of view. From a methodological perspective, this research is rooted in Mode 2 paradigm, developing knowledge in the application context to address practical issues while mobilizing various theoretical perspectives and methodologies (Gibbons et al., 1994). It relies on a hybrid methodology at the intersection of action research (Shani & Coghlan, 2021b) and design science research (Collatto et al., 2018).

Shani and Coghlan (2018, p. 4) define action research as,

> An emergent inquiry process in which applied behavioral science knowledge is integrated with existing organizational knowledge and applied to address real organizational issue. It is simultaneously concerned with bringing about change in organizations, in developing self-help competencies in organizational members and

> in adding to scientific knowledge. Finally, it is an evolving process that is undertaken in a spirit of collaboration and co-inquiry.

Action research can thus be considered an emergent inquiry process that brings together behavioral science knowledge and existing organizational knowledge to solve real organizational problems (Coghlan, 2011) and achieve rigorous and significant results in a truly collaborative approach (Rapoport, 1970; Pasmore et al., 2008). Scholars usually play a dual role as researcher and agent of change (Roth et al., 2007). This gives them the opportunity to produce knowledge in its application context (MacLean et al., 2002), a data-driven approach that allows them to apply experimental and unobtrusive methodologies, test causality, identify the mechanisms underlying the identified relationships, and finally, co-evaluate their robustness through collaborative interpretation (Pasmore et al., 2008).

Central to the action research approach is addressing real organizational needs (Shani & Coghlan, 2018). We work in close collaboration with companies in defining the challenge that the research platform will address. The second key aspect is the link with existing behavioral science knowledge to address the needs of organizations through a rigorous research approach. In this project, a team of researchers is dedicated to exploring the multiple facets of the organizational problem, highlighting the dominant approaches in the academic literature that can provide insights for a solution. The collaborative aspect of our research entails multiple interactions and exchanges among the various stakeholders: all partners interact in multiple meetings in which common challenges are shared, discussed, and themes identified. Moreover, each partner interacts with the research team independently to gain a thorough understanding of the specific organizational challenge.

The development of this solution requires a more hands-on approach and follows the design science research directives. Collatto and colleagues (2018) define design science research (DSR) as,

> Design science research is a research method that seeks to generate knowledge on designing an artifact or even presenting a solution (…) it helps to draw close researchers and members of organizations in order to generate useful knowledge to solve real problems (…) it enables the production of research in several disciplinary areas (…) it provides a systematic procedure that guides the construction of studies aiming to design artifacts (…) it is concerned with performing an evaluation to develop artifacts (…) its objective is not developing an optimal solution, but rather a

> satisfactory solution compared to existing ones (…) the solutions generated should be capable of generalization to a certain class of problems.

DSR has its roots in the field of information systems (Gregor & Hevner, 2013), but its relevance is becoming more generally accepted (Kuechler & Vaishnavi, 2008; Hevner & Chatterjee, 2010). DSR is based on the construction of different socio-technical artifacts to evaluate information systems and the impact of change interventions. In other words, it builds on the design-science paradigm aiming to extend human and organizational knowledge by creating innovative artifacts (Hevner et al., 2004). Through DSR, the researcher endeavors to create knowledge through physical interventions on the artifacts with proposals that will have an impact on human behaviors or organizational dynamics.

We adopt design science research to develop a set of organizational artifacts that can help the organizational sensemaking process. The development of this artifact requires the research team to enter into the organizational dynamics and connect these to external kernel theories. In contrast to most academic approaches to knowledge production, through DSR, the research team does not only study the artifacts used within an organization – as in the case of Stigliani and Ravasi's (2012) study – but actively contributes to creating a set of tools it deems useful. The artifact is then tested in the organization, and the researchers can develop knowledge about its usage.

This project does not adopt either a pure action research or pure design science research approach, but each partner represents a hybrid research embedded in Mode 2 research paradigm. At the collective platform level, the artifact is developed through design science research.

4 A hybrid approach to research

Our hybrid approach can be described as a three-phase process where each phase entails specific interactions with each of the partners and a different role for the research team. Figure 3.1 illustrates the hybrid process.

The first phase is "defining the scope and hypotheses" whereby the research team defines the overall goal of the research project. Building on theories and prior research, the team also defines the assumptions and hypotheses to be tested in the research project and designs an experience to perform the tests in real organizations. Once companies

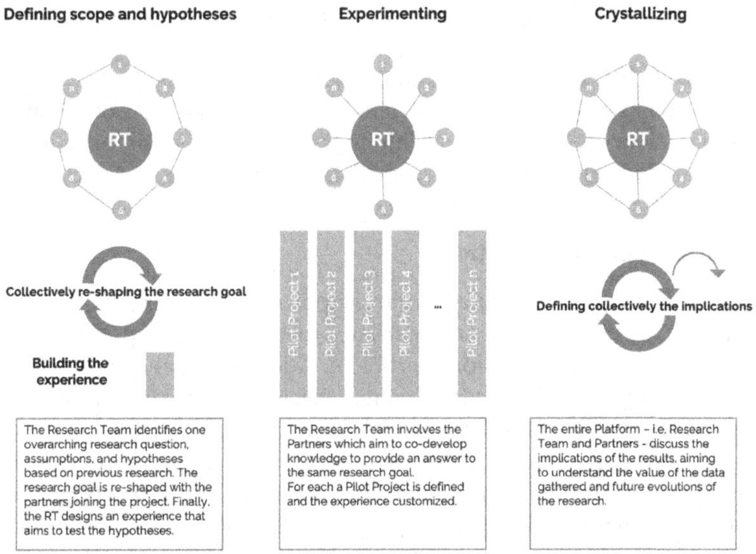

Figure 3.1 The research phases.
Source: Our own elaboration.

are involved, the project kicks off. In this phase, the research team presents the project's overall research goal and main assumptions. Nevertheless, the research team and all partners collectively reframe the overall project goal and research questions to ensure their relevance for all parties involved and a meaningful goal for the research project.

The second phase, "reframing and experimenting", focuses on the concrete actions that the research team must undertake in collaboration with each of the partner companies. The research team works singularly with each partner on a pilot project that aims to refine and test the hypotheses in their respective setting, working on actual innovation projects. Due to the constraints and the particular needs of each company, the experience is partly customized. In other words, within the same structure, each partner has a specific experience aiming to gather additional data that may be valuable for the organization, or test additional hypotheses relevant to each particular setting.

The third and final phase, "crystallizing", takes place after the research team's analysis of all the data gathered in the various experiences. All partners are provided with the results of the overall research project. The entire community then discusses the implications of these results to gain insights from the data collected. These interactions also aim to allow the hidden opportunities and challenges to emerge during the research project, extremely valuable to identify the goal of the subsequent edition of the research project.

Based on this cycle, a new experience – the storymakers workshop – is designed. In the following, we highlight the set of design principles that guide the definition of the storymaking experience.

5 The storymaking practice

In line with the design science research approach (Hevner et al., 2004), the research team designs an experience involving participants working on a specific organizational problem. A longitudinal experience is developed through which participants reflect on their views of organizational change and the personal transformation process. Design tools are developed specifically for this storymaking experience to support writing and critically reflecting on the transformation story. Next, we introduce some underlying principles that drive the experience, drawing on the literature and inspirational case studies, and then describe the process and activities undertaken.

5.1 From organizational stories to human stories

Companies share innovation stories to communicate their ideology and value to people (DeLarge, 2004). Some popular examples bear witness to this. In 1955, Disneyland was founded. The Walt Disney amusement park was considered one of the greatest entrepreneurial risks in American business history, and today hosts millions of visitors every year. Disneyland exemplifies a success story that has led Walt Disney to collect billions of dollars in revenue (Beltrami, 2017). Similarly, the launch of the Apple iMac in 1988 is still praised as the rebirth of the Apple brand (Verganti, 2009).

Stories become memorable when they touch people's inner feelings and emotions, when they are able to emphasize them, and when they are human (Cunliffe & Coupland, 2012). Through stories, Walt Disney shares its dream of a place where children and adults have fun together. At Apple, stories tell the visionary relationship between Steve Jobs and Jonathan Ive.

Throughout the years, researchers have found that stories about people are more meaningful to an audience than the mere communication of data and facts (Green & Brock, 2000; Barraza et al., 2015). The purpose of storymaking is to engage and enable individuals to understand and embrace a new organizational direction, empathizing with the necessary change (Blomquist & Lundin, 2010; Enninga & van der Lugt, 2016). Therefore, the first principle consists in engaging them in creating not the story of an organization, but a human story.

5.2 From human stories to personal stories

Researchers refer to experience-taking as the immersive phenomenon of assuming the character's identity, which can also drive people to change their perceptions and behaviors (Livingstone, 1988; Cohen, 2001; Kaufman & Libby, 2012). Central to the idea of experience-taking is the concept of letting go of one's own identity and accepting the character's subjective experience. Stories can carry us to a different point in time and space, leading us to see the world through the eyes of someone with different characteristics to our own. For example, when we think of the abductive reasoning of detective Sherlock Holmes, we are transported in our thoughts to 19th century London. When we read about the adventures of little Frodo Baggins who sets out to save his home from evil and destruction, we take part in the nine companions' journey across Middle-earth. When at last Frodo returns home, he is a changed person, and so is the reader who has lived the same adventures, fought the same battles, and experienced the same bravery.

When we are absorbed by a story, we don't consciously project ourselves onto the character who at that moment is living a different experience. Perspective-taking means changing the perception of the self and assuming another's thoughts or emotions. Experience-taking is different in that the self-concept is left behind in order to adopt the feelings and emotions of another (Kaufman & Libby, 2012).

For this reason, the second principle of the storymaking practice is to drive future behaviors by means of experience-taking where people put themselves at the center of the organizational change process. Rather than a story about the collective of individuals doing something, the story should be about a precise individual who lives adventures and needs to overcome barriers to change. The organizational transformation comes second, as people need to transform themselves first (Chandler & Torbert, 2003; Coghlan & Shani, 2021). Leveraging the realistic narratives perspective, people make a story of their own change (e.g. beliefs, skills, and behaviors) and commit to take coherent action. The next step describes how individual stories of change coalesce in organizational transformation.

5.3 From personal stories to organizational stories

Organizations are dynamic entities that continuously update their purpose (Gray et al., 1985). The sensemaking literature extensively describes innovation as the collective act of making sense of things (Weick, 1995; Maitlis & Christianson, 2014). Change occurs when individuals transform collectively (García-Morales et al., 2006).

Today, innovative technologies and entertainment platforms offer us unpublished ways in which narratives can support the actualization of modern communities. Popular TV shows like *Game of Thrones*, *The Walking Dead*, or *Orange is the New Black* are compelling examples of stories where the entanglement of a multitude of diverse characters' storylines gives rise to the whole plot. Here, the concept of the fractal story emerges (Boje, 2015): within an adaptive system, story webs coalesce around a common goal, while change stems from the overall interweaving. George Orwell's *Animal Farm* illustrates this model.

Similarly, individual stories that move around the same plot form an overall organizational story. Consider poor Frodo Baggins and the battle of good over evil that was not won by him and his companions alone. Throughout several 100 pages, the stories that lead to the end result are multiple: each of the nine initial companions pursues their own trajectory, and while moving together with the others some of time, in the end each story is different.

The idea of individual stories that form an organizational narrative is similar. Each individual is part of the whole organization, each goes back every day to their job and interacts with colleagues, and each receives the same stimuli both from the external environment and from management. Thus, although everybody's change trajectory differs, the daily interactions and exchanges give rise to the overall evolution of the whole organization.

The third storymaking principle aims to capture the richness of diversity and the emergence of a collective narrative. As the third storymaking principle, through empowering the creation of fractal narratives via co-creation, we aim to achieve a compelling effect whereby the set of interactions among all employees' stories (micro-narratives) constitute the single organizational story (macro-narrative).

5.4 Building the storyworld

Even if individuals develop their own interpretation of change, this freedom takes place within well-defined organizational boundaries. For example, in Gioia and Chittipeddi's (1991) study of the strategic changes in a large university introduced by the arrival of a new president, the frame within which the strategic change took place was well defined by changes in the market and the president's interpretation thereof. Similarly, the change process that Lüscher and Lewis (2008) witnessed at Lego was initiated and framed by the top management's strategic objectives.

However, stories cannot develop freely. Before individual stories can develop into an overarching plot, and individual voices give rise to a choral evolution, the locus needs to be defined.

The presentation of a storyworld takes place at the beginning of the macro narrative, and even if unnoticed by the reader, it draws the boundaries around the locus where the story will take place. *Worldbuilding* is the process of constructing a complete and plausible imaginary world that serves as the context for a story. Embedded within foresight and design practices, worldbuilding describes the creation of contextual rules that define a larger reality (von Stackelberg & McDowell, 2015). For example, the opening sequence of every film in George Lucas' Star Wars series illustrates the backstory and context of the *galaxy far, far away*. Similarly, the design of the technological and socio-political features of the world preceded the action in Steven Spielbierg's *Minority Report* (McDowell, 2019).

Once the storyworld has been defined, the characters appear to develop naturally. While maintaining freedom, they now are bound by the limits of their world. In the organizational setting, managers are free to develop the world in which they want the organization to move. What management cannot do though is define how people will move in this direction. Therefore, the fourth and final storymaking principle is setting the boundaries of the storyworld, i.e., the fundamentals of the vision and the elements to avoid in pursuing the vision. Thereafter, individuals are free to shape their own stories.

6 Designing a storymaking experience

Based on these principles, we designed a longitudinal experience to guide the sensemaking process. To do so, we relied on a set of cards (the story-coach) to help participants write their own stories and embrace organizational change through personal transformation. We designed a set of the card to facilitate the writing process, while leveraging on the main elements of the hero's journey by Campbell (1949). The cards are described in Table 3.1 and introduced throughout the process in the next paragraphs.

Table 3.1 The story-coach card set

Cards	*Description*
My self	To write a meaningful transformation story, the organizational transformation needs to be re-positioned at the individual level.
My reason to leave	Motivation and aspiration affect the individual tendency to change and innovate. Therefore, each story should highlight the personal motivation to embrace the transformation journey.
My direction	When innovating, individuals should have a clear vision of where they are going. Hence, everyone should set a personal trajectory to envision how their story can fit into the overall challenge.
My contribution	To engage people in innovation, it is important to identify a concrete output to work on. Hence, stories should translate personal aspirations for transformation into concrete contributions.
Obstacle	Innovation deals with uncertainty, therefore obstacles will emerge on the way. Every story should have a series of trials to shape the transformation of individuals.
Sacrificial moment	Along with obstacles, transformation implies letting go of previous conceptions and meanings. Hence, stories should help accepting the sacrifice of something dear to succeed in the journey.
Companion	Innovation is easier done with someone else. Therefore, stories should support individuals in identifying a companion to accomplish their transformation.
Mentor	Transformation deals with evolution and change. Therefore, transformation stories should have an expert in the field to instruct, guide, or lead individuals throughout their quest.
Object	As any story, transformation journeys may require physical objects as a support. Stories can benefit of physical tools or artifacts to be used during the transformation.
My commitment	The first step toward understanding an innovation opportunity consists in taking action. Transformation stories are prospective and should be progressively realized through small, concrete actions selected by individuals to commit to their goals.
Enhancement	Constructive criticism can foster creative idea generation among peers in innovation. Hence, stories should help individuals sharing knowledge and contributing to enriching the ideas of others.
Criticism	Innovation is prospective but anchored in sensemaking of past events. Hence, intimate moments of self-perception help to reframe interpretation of the course of events and upcoming chapters.

Table 3.2 The brief for each partner

Partner	*The brief*
Nestlè	How can you be recognized as an innovative leader?
Philips	How can you be recognized as a partner for the development of modular and configurable solutions?
Sasol	What is your personal commitment to using 10% of your time to foster innovation?
Sintetica	How do you need to change – and what do you have to learn to do – to take advantage of digital opportunities while remaining at the center?
Sorgenia	How should I change my daily behaviors to make our company's new meaning real in my daily work?
STEF	How do you need to change – and what do you have to learn to do – to exploit the potential of the new work model and increase time-to-market (TTM) performance?

First, the storyworld is jointly defined by the company and the research team (Table 3.2) consisting of three main elements:

- ***The brief***: The challenge participants are encouraged to embrace.
- ***The pillars of the transformation***: Three or four organizational values (principles and opportunities) participants should maintain in framing their stories.
- ***The things that can be left behind***: Three or four organizational values that may not be appropriate in the new context.

For each organization, 20–25 participants attended four workshops (the story episodes) over three months (see Table 3.3). In each episode, individuals began by reflecting on their own transformation before sharing their thoughts with a partner. Then, participants were asked to write their narrative on a virtual "piece of paper", building the three chapters that would define their whole story of individual transformation. After reading their stories to each other, they identified a set of keywords – or shared principles – that emerged from their narratives and represent their shared vision.

Throughout the process, participants use cards to make notes of their reflections before writing down their stories (Figure 3.2). This story-coach card set helps participants reflect on their transformation process in a structured way, devoting their attention to some specific aspects to first frame their transformation and then review their progress in the subsequent episodes. These cards are used as a canvas on which participants draw or make notes as they design the plot of their

Table 3.3 The main steps of the process

Episodes	*Main activities and outcomes*
Kick Off	The storyworld is introduced to participants who are invited to start reflecting on what they need to be able to embrace it. They start by defining their personal direction and the skills, capabilities, and tools needed for the journey.
Episode 1	Participants reflect on all the elements they might need to embrace their personal transformation journey (e.g., a companion, a mentor, or a tool) and identify the potential obstacles or hurdles they might face. After defining their story, they share it with a sparring partner who contributes to their reflections. In addition, they define the first commitment they aim to complete to get closer to their personal direction. Finally, the first episode is written and shared in a small circle.
Episodes 2 and 3	Participants start with retrospective self-reflection on the outcome of the commitment made. They critically reflect on what they learned and the challenges faced, e.g., additional obstacles or hurdles, missing skills or tools, as well as whether their own direction needs to be updated. Finally, they make a new commitment, write the episode, and shared it in a small circle.
Episode 4	The results of the experiences are presented to the participants and the leadership team. The researchers, participants, and managers critically reflect on what they have learned and the impact of the journey for them as individuals and for the organization as a whole.

story before writing it down as text. The following is a brief description of each episode of the storymaking experience.

6.1 Episode 0: Envisioning the transformation

Episode 0 is the starting point of the transformation journey where participants gather their ideas before starting their adventure. First, participants reflect on their own characteristics and choose an objective for their transformation: this should be relevant but non-urgent, so that everyone can pursue their objectives over the following months. The cards of the first episode address both the person and the outcome of the change.

The first cards supporting reflection are related to the participants themselves. The card *Myself* helps them think about their own characteristics, define who they are, and which characteristics they wish

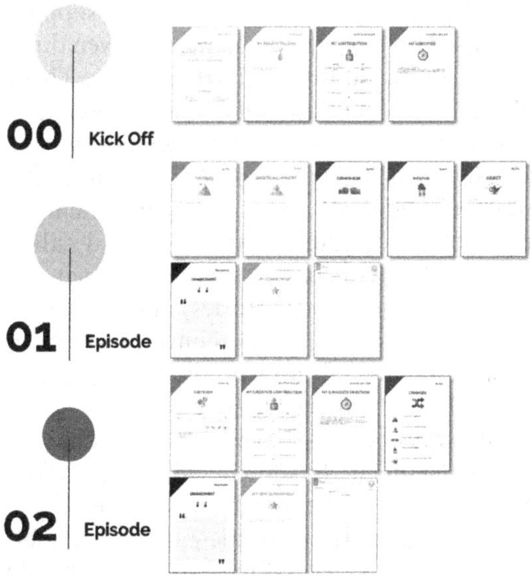

Figure 3.2 The storymaking experience and card set.
Source: Our own elaboration.

to leverage throughout the journey. The second card represents their individual motivation: *My Reason to Leave* spurs reasoning on the rationale for transforming personally. The *About My Future Self* cards (*My Contribution* and *My Direction*) support reasoning on the transformation outcome and help in defining how the change should happen, designing their vision of the transformation and its impact on their job. These cards can then be revised in later episodes if necessary.

6.2 Episode 1: Designing the transformation

In the first episode, participants design their whole transformation journey for the first time and reflect on its critical aspects. To support these reflections, cards related to the *Plot* of the narratives are at their disposal. Two cards are mandatory in the stories: the *Obstacle* card represents something that might hinder the process, as identifying this aspect early can help participants understand how to overcome it. The *Sacrificial Moment* card describes a moment in which they would need to give something up, helping to understand that transformation represents growth but may require a sacrifice.

Furthermore, transformation as a process might require support from some additional elements. Therefore, participants are given three optional cards they can use to provide texture to their story. These cards represent the possibility of relying on an *Object*, any physical or digital tool that might prove useful during the journey, identifying one or more *Companions*, colleagues, or friends they desire to share the transformation path with, or a *Mentor*, an expert providing guidance.

After writing their story so far, one further card is added called *Enhancement*, which represents the feedback of a sparring partner. All participants get together in pairs, share their stories, and receive an external perspective of their transformation. This conversation in an intimate environment allows critically reflecting on the story.

Next, the last card is provided to make a concrete commitment to action. Through the *My Commitment* card, participants define one specific action they commit to completing in the subsequent weeks – before the next episode – to begin working on their transformation journey.

Once all the cards have been completed, participants write their narratives on a dedicated card. The storymaking experience should ultimately lead to the creation of individual transformation stories. Having the narratives in front of them in written form helps make the story vivid instead of a collage of separate elements.

As the last step, the whole group together draws a summary of the individual stories. This is the actual moment in which the individual narratives coalesce to form a broader picture. First, participants share their stories in the group, reading them out aloud, after this, they synthesize their stories in a number of principles. These principles represent the values that all the stories have in common.

6.3 Episodes 2–3

In the subsequent episodes, participants go back to the stories written previously and make sense of the changes in their professional lives. Thereafter, they have the possibility to edit and change the stories they have written so that they more accurately reflect their future path.

The starting point of these reflections is the *Criticism* card through which they reflect on the level of achievement of the commitment made in the previous episode. Reflecting on the level of advancement informs their reflections on the story, as participants realize whether they will need to change their future steps.

Thereafter, individuals pursue the same reflections as in the first iteration. They are provided with a set of cards that allows updating their previous reflections both on the story direction and the plot. Again, stories are enhanced by a partner, and culminate in the commitment to new action before the story is written down. This is the second episode of the personal transformation journey.

Each of the episodes terminates in the same group reflection, as individuals share their stories by reading them to each other and defining three group-level principles.

During the experiments, we gathered all the participants' stories and interactions. This enabled us to explore how both the individual and collective stories were framed. In addition to analyzing the commitments and their achievement, the level of engagement and the perception of meaningfulness enabled us to explore how the transformation took place and how everyone contributed.

7 Empirical setting

During this research, we held over 25 workshops in 75 sessions (the follow-up episodes took place in smaller, parallel sessions) with partner companies to investigate the role of storymaking practices in fostering transformation. During these workshops, all data related to the material produced by participants were collected and analyzed. In addition to the analysis of the written content, several questionnaires were submitted to participants in the workshops. The data gathered included the perceived meaningfulness of their transformation project, their engagement in the project, and the actual concrete actions undertaken toward their transformation goal.

Meaningfulness is the value that participants attribute in their written stories. Bellis and Verganti (2021) developed a scale to assess the extent to which individuals feel their sensemaking process has led to a meaningful output. In particular, we assess the degree to which the stories are perceived as *plausible, promising, compelling*, and *effective*.

As for *engagement*, we measured participants' emotional engagement in the project to assess the extent to which the project has been understood and accepted throughout the organization (Garcia Martinez, 2015; Figure 3.3).

The research is also built on the stories that participants wrote throughout the workshops to offer a visualization of the stories in a summarized way, wordclouds and text mining have been used to elaborate the figures presented in the next chapter. These analyses are presented and described also from a methodological perspective in Chapter 5.

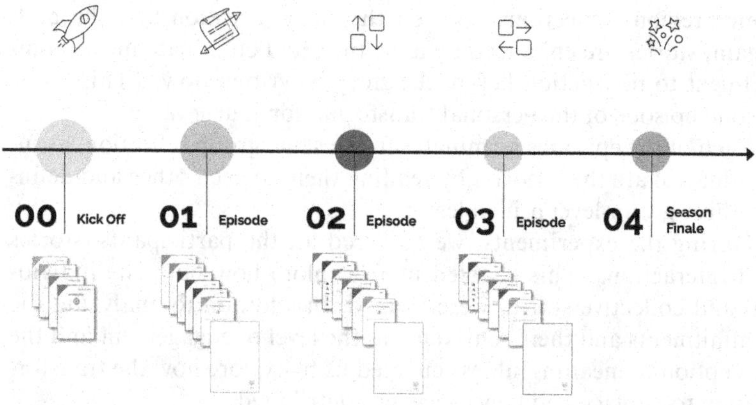

Figure 3.3 Workshop structure for each partner company.
Source: Our own elaboration.

8 Our project as a research platform

Our research approach affords value to three different stakeholder groups. First, for participants in the workshops, the three-month experience allows them to deal with change that would otherwise have disrupted their way of working. Second, for the organizations taking part, this project provides clarity concerning the objectives of the transformation process while helping design a new way of organizing that is not simply defined top-down, but considers the bottom-up reflections of employees. Last, for the research team, the data gathered in these workshops (from textual and visual story data, qualitative interviews, quantitative measures of engagement and meaningfulness, to name but a few) are relevant for various studies, each connecting some of the aspects observed. We can view the output of the data gathering process as a cube: slicing the cube in different ways means adopting a different perspective of the observations, thus leading to different potential research streams.

For these reasons, our project can be described as a research platform: the project is only the central infrastructure in the form of workshops that provide value to different users and positive externalities. The more companies that are part of the platform, the greater and more meaningful the data, since the questions can be better defined and more general in application. Research that addresses these meaningful questions in turn becomes more attractive for other companies to join the platform. Moreover, once this approach is shown to help individuals make sense of change, their willingness to partake increases. This has been demonstrated by companies that have been part of the project for more than one year: individuals who had taken part in a previous experiment returned, and many new individuals joined after positive referrals from their colleagues.

The workshop structure exemplifies a research platform in the sense that once a basic structure has been built, many derivatives (in this case, research) can be developed (Gawer & Cusumano, 2014; Trabucchi & Magistretti, 2020). Therefore, in addition to the overall question on the role of storymaking in organizational transformation, other derivative research directions emerged and were explored. Indeed, throughout the process, various aspects enabled the research team to gather additional data that nurture other research streams, both for surveys or activities, such as pair reflection or the final sharing in groups. In particular, this research platform has triggered three vertical research areas and research questions that are presented and explored in Chapter 5:

1 Intimacy in innovation

Working in pairs is emerging as a powerful practice to foster innovation. Pairs are the smallest unit beyond individuals with the valuable characteristic of leveraging intimacy that is difficult to achieve in a team. Various sessions in which individuals work in pairs explore the role of intimacy in engaging people and developing meaningful transformations.

2 Convergence in a shared direction

The experience focuses on individual transformations that all begin from a single brief or challenge defined by the organization. There are a number of ways to help people converge when developing innovation or working on a new direction. With various individuals working on the same transformation process, data on how they converge and how they react to each other's stories are explored to link them with the main variables observed in the study.

3 Cognition and transformation

We all differ in the way we approach things, how we make sense of innovation and how we react to change and take action. The engagement process activated through storymaking might be linked to the rational or intuitive cognitive approach. As we dig into our preferred approach to innovation, our language expresses our thoughts that evolve throughout the transformation process.

These three vertical research streams enhance the value of the research platform, providing the opportunity to explore other meaningful

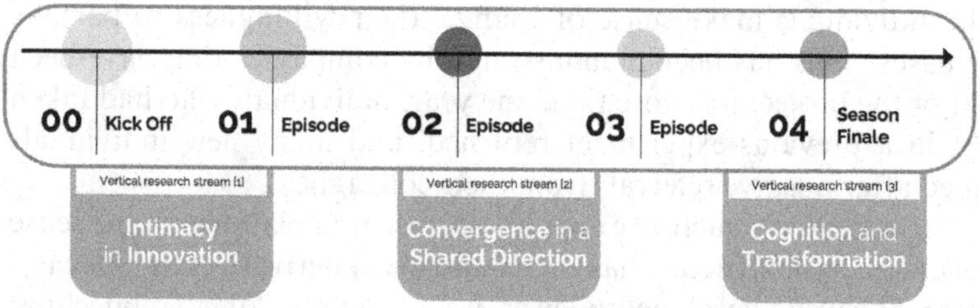

Figure 3.4 The research platform.

questions at the intersection of innovation, design, and leadership (Figure 3.4).

References

Barraza, J. A., Alexander, V., Beavin, L. E., Terris, E. T., & Zak, P. J. (2015). The heart of the story: Peripheral physiology during narrative exposure predicts charitable giving. *Biological Psychology*, 105, 138–143.

Bellis, P., & Verganti, R. (2021). Pairs as pivots of innovation: How collaborative sensemaking benefits from innovating in twos. *Innovation*, 23(3), 375–399.

Beltrami, E. (2017). The cineteca del Friuli at 40. *Journal of Film Preservation*, 97, 94–98.

Blomquist, T., & Lundin, R. A. (2010). Projects – real, virtual or what? *International Journal of Managing Projects in Business*, 3(1), 10–21.

Boje, D. M. (2015). Mapping quantum storytelling fractal patterns before and beneath triple bottom line's and veterans administration's stupid narratives. Available at https://davidboje.com/quantum/pdfs_Proceedings_BigStory_2015/What%20is%20Quantum%20Storytelling.pdf

Campbell, J. (1949). *The hero with a thousand faces*. New York: Pantheon.

Chandler, D., & Torbert, W. (2003). Transforming inquiry and action. *Action Inquiry*, 1(2), 133–152.

Coghlan, D. (2011). Action research: Exploring perspectives on a philosophy of practical knowing. *Academy of Management Annals*, 5(1), 53–87.

Coghlan, D., & Shani, A. B. (Rami). (2021). Abductive reasoning as the integrating mechanism between First-Second-and Third-Person practice in action research. *Systematic Practice and Action Research*, 34, 463–474.

Coghlan, D., Shani, A. B. (Rami), & Dahm, P. (2020). Knowledge production in organization development. *Journal of Change Management*, 20(1), 81–98.

Coghlan, D., Shani, A. B. R., & Hay, G. W. (2019). Toward a social science philosophy of organization development and change. *Research in Organizational Change and Development*, 27, 1–29.

Cohen, J. (2001). Defining identification: A theoretical look at the identification of audiences with media characters. *Mass Communication & Society*, 4(3), 245–264.

Collatto, D. C., Dresch, A., Lacerda, D. P., & Bentz, I. G. (2018). Is action design research indeed necessary? Analysis and synergies between action research and design science research. *Systemic Practice and Action Research*, 31(3), 239–267.

Cunliffe, A., & Coupland, C. (2012). From hero to villain to hero: Making experience sensible through embodied narrative sensemaking. *Human Relations*, 65(1), 63–88.

DeLarge, C. (2004). Storytelling as a critical success factor in design processes and outcomes. *Design Management Review*, 15, 76–81.

Enninga, T., & van der Lugt, R. (2016). The innovation journey and the skipper of the raft: About the role of narratives in innovation project leadership. *Project Management Journal*, 47(2), 103–114.

Garcia Martinez, M. (2015). Solver engagement in knowledge sharing in crowdsourcing communities: Exploring the link to creativity. *Research Policy*, 44(8), 1419–1430.

García-Morales, V. J., Moreno, A. R., & Lloréns-Montes, F. J. (2006). Strategic capabilities and their effects on performance: Entrepreneurial, learning, innovator and problematic SMEs. *International Journal of Management and Enterprise Development*, 3(3), 191–211.

Gawer, A., & Cusumano, M. A. (2014). Industry platforms and ecosystem innovation. *Journal of Product Innovation Management*, 31(3), 417–433.

Gibbons, M., Limoges, C., Nowotny, H., Schwartzman, S., Scott, P., & Trow, M. (1994). *The new production of knowledge: The dynamics of science and research in contemporary societies*. London: Sage.

Gibbons, M., Limoges, C., & Scott, P. (2011). Revisiting Mode 2 at Noors Slott. *Prometheus*, 29(4), 361–372.

Gioia, D. A., & Chittipeddi, K. (1991). Sensemaking and sensegiving in strategic change initiation. *Strategic Management Journal*, 12(6), 433–448.

Gray, B., Bougon, M. G., & Donnellon, A. (1985). Organizations as constructions and destructions of meaning. *Journal of Management*, 11(2), 83–98.

Green, M. C., & Brock, T. C. (2000). The role of transportation in the persuasiveness of public narratives. *Journal of Personality and Social Psychology*, 79(5), 701–721.

Gregor, S., & Hevner, A. R. (2013). Positioning and presenting design science research for maximum impact. *MIS Quarterly: Management Information Systems*, 37(2), 337–355.

Hevner, A., & Chatterjee, S. (2010). Design science research in information systems. In Hevner, A., & Chatterjee, S. (Eds.), *Design research in information systems*. Integrated Series in Information Systems (pp. 9–22). Boston, MA: Springer.

Hevner, A. R., March, S. T., Park, J., & Ram, S. (2004). Design science in information systems research. *MIS Quarterly: Management Information Systems*, 28(1), 75–105.

Kaufman, G. F., & Libby, L. K. (2012). Changing beliefs and behavior through experience-taking. *Journal of Personality and Social Psychology*, 103(1), 1–19.

Kuechler, B., & Vaishnavi, V. (2008). On theory development in design science research: Anatomy of a research project. *European Journal of Information Systems*, 17(5), 489–504.

Livingstone, M. S. (1988). Art, illusion and the visual system. *Scientific American*, 258(1), 78–85.

Lüscher, L. S., & Lewis, M. W. (2008). Organizational change and managerial sensemaking: Working through paradox. *Academy of Management Journal*, 51(2), 221–240.

MacIntosh, R., Mason, K., Beech, N., & Bartunek, J. (2021). *Delivering impact in management research*. Oxon: Routledge.

MacLean, D., MacIntosh, R., & Grant, S. (2002). Mode 2 management research. *British Journal of Management*, 13(3), 189–207.

Maitlis, S., & Christianson, M. (2014). Sensemaking in organizations: Taking stock and moving forward. *Academy of Management Annals*, 8(1), 57–125.

McDowell, A. (2019). Storytelling shapes the future. *Journal of Futures Studies*, 23(3), 105–112.

Meynell, H. A. (1998). *Redirecting philosophy: Reflections on the nature of knowledge from Plato to Lonergan*. Toronto: University of Toronto Press.

Mirvis, P., Mohrman, S., & Worley, C. (2021). *How to do relevant research*. Cheltenham: Elgar.

Nowotny, H., Scott, P. B., & Gibbons, M. T. (2001). *Re-thinking science: Knowledge and the public in an age of uncertainty* (1st edition). New York: Wiley.

Pasmore, W. A., Stymne, B., Shani, A. B. (Rami), Mohrman, S. A., & Adler, N. (2008). The promise of collaborative management research. In Shani, A. B. (Rami), Mohrman, S. A., Pasmore, W., Stymne, B., & Adler, N. (Eds.), *Handbook of collaborative management research* (pp. 7–31). Thousand Oaks, CA: Sage.

Rapoport, R. N. (1970). Three dilemmas in action research: With special reference to the Tavistock experience. *Human Relations*, 23(6), 499–513.

Roth, J., Shani, A. B. (Rami), & Leary, M. M. (2007). Insider action research: Facing the challenges of new capability development within a biopharma company. *Action Research*, 5(1), 41–60.

Shani, A. B. (Rami), & Coghlan, D. (2018). Enhancing action, research, and collaboration in organization development. *Organization Development Journal*, 36(3), 37–43.

Shani, A. B. (Rami), & Coghlan, D. (2021a). *Collaborative inquiry for organization development and change*. Cheltenham: Elgar.

Shani, A. B. (Rami), & Coghlan, D. (2021b). Action research in business and management: A reflective review. *Action Research*, 19(3), 518–541.

Stigliani, I., & Ravasi, D. (2012). Organizing thoughts and connecting brains: Material practices and the transition from individual to group-level prospective sensemaking. *Academy of Management Journal*, 55(5), 1232–1259.

Trabucchi, D., & Magistretti, S. (2020). The battle of superheroes: The rise of the knowledge platform strategy in the movie industry. *Journal of Knowledge Management*, 24(8), 1881–1898.

Verganti, R. (2009). *Design driven innovation: Changing the rules of competition by radically innovating what things mean*. Boston, MA: Harvard Business Press.

von Stackelberg, P., & McDowell, A. (2015). What in the world? Storyworlds, science fiction, and futures studies. *Journal of Futures Studies*, 20(2), 25–46.

Weick, K. E. (1995). *Sensemaking in organizations (foundations for organizational science)*. Thousand Oaks: Sage Publications.

4 The Transformation Stories

1 Nestlé: becoming innovative leaders

Nestlé is a global leader in the food sector aiming to enhance and contribute to the quality of life and a healthier future. Based in Switzerland since 1866, today Nestlé has six business lines, 2,000+ brands, and 308,000 employees. With these numbers, the challenge of engaging people in innovation is something of a hurdle.

In recent years, the company has greatly progressed in creating a common innovation culture and a shared way of thinking about innovation and solving problems creatively. In collaboration and co-design with Nestlé's Global Program Lead for Management and Executive Capability Building, the IT Innovation Methodologies team, one of six teams in the global R&D and IT Innovation unit, covers all innovation stages under Nestlé's Global IT function. The Innovation Methodologies' mission is to empower the business and employees with the most relevant innovation methodologies that foster greater value to support its innovation vision. The team has four priorities:

1 *Innovation as a service:* The team connects, facilitates, mentors, and co-creates tailor-made innovation solutions (HOW) by identifying and applying the latest and most relevant innovation methods (WHAT).
2 *Innovation academy*: The team is an in-house knowledge partner that designs and facilitates learning-by-doing experiences. The Innovation Academy combines high-quality top-end industry standards with internal expertise to tackle the dynamic uncertainty and complexity of today's fast-changing environment to ensure consumer-centric products, increased agility, and speed to market for long-term business growth.

DOI: 10.4324/9781003276210–4

3 *Innovation tools*: Supporting the innovation culture and accelerating Nestlé's digital transformation, the tools consist in democratizing innovation and building employee and businesses innovation practices into everyday life to make the innovative mindset an integral part of how Nestlé works.
4 *Innovation ecosystems*: Creating the conditions that allow human creativity and curiosity to thrive in diverse communities with internal and external partners.

Nestlé launched a call to innovation enthusiasts to take part in the storymaking experience.

1.1 The challenge

Nestlé aimed to engage innovation enthusiasts by reflecting on innovative leadership and asking people to embrace a personal transformation journey.

We live in a world where there are plenty of stimuli and innovation opportunities, and thus being recognized as an innovative leader is becoming more and more challenging. How can people be recognized as innovative leaders?

Relying on the storymaking experience, the participants designed stories that would lead to their recognition as innovative leaders, thinking about the way, the people, and the moments that would enable this. Twenty participants embraced this initiative.

1.2 The storymaker workshop

1.2.1 Setting the storyworld

The Nestlé and research core teams worked together to craft the storyworld for this transformation journey, finding a way to challenge those who wanted to join the research quest and set the boundaries of the stories they wrote.

The Brief: We live in a world awash with ideas and opportunities. Digital media continually propose new ideas, and digital technologies potentially offer a multitude of opportunities. Nevertheless, picking the right idea is a huge challenge, and even more so building meaningful relationships with those in the organization fostering innovation. Hence the question: *How can you be recognized as an innovative leader?*

The Pillars: The Nestlé leadership and the research teams jointly identified three fundamental elements characterizing innovative leaders and their transformation journey, thus pivotal in crafting the participant's stories:

- *Innovative leaders protect teams.* This first pillar highlights the strong community culture that is needed to foster innovation. Leaders need to protect their teams and help them grow.
- *They don't do innovation; they help others do it.* Fostering innovation is not an easy task and innovative leaders are ready to help others in this process.
- *Brave enough to go where no one else has gone to show new opportunities.* Innovative leaders are keen to explore new territories and present the opportunities to others (Figure 4.1).

What can be left behind: Finally, the Nestlé and the research core teams jointly defined a set of common pitfalls of innovative leaders that should not be part of the transformation journey:

- *Sharing knowledge just to share knowledge (overwhelming information).* Many people tend to show their knowledge by simply sharing it with anyone, even without context. This attitude is detrimental to innovation, leading to inertia rather action.
- *Wrong communication.* To be recognized as innovative leaders, people often impose their knowledge and show it off, thereby

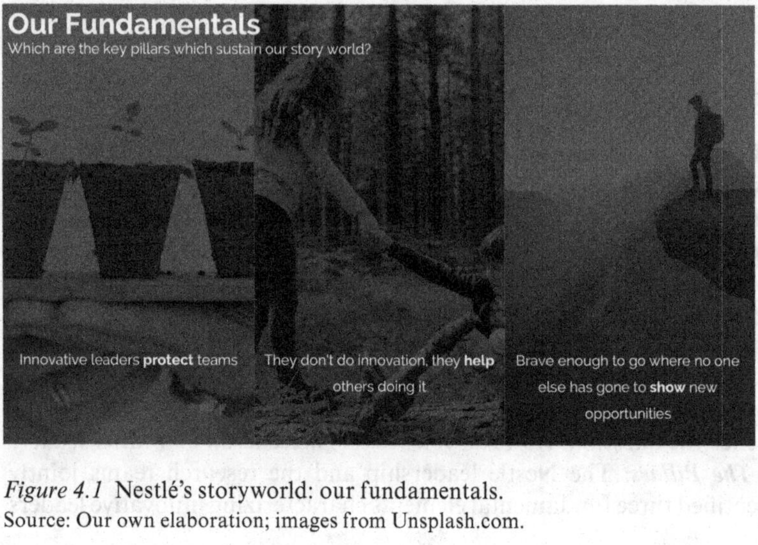

Figure 4.1 Nestlé's storyworld: our fundamentals.
Source: Our own elaboration; images from Unsplash.com.

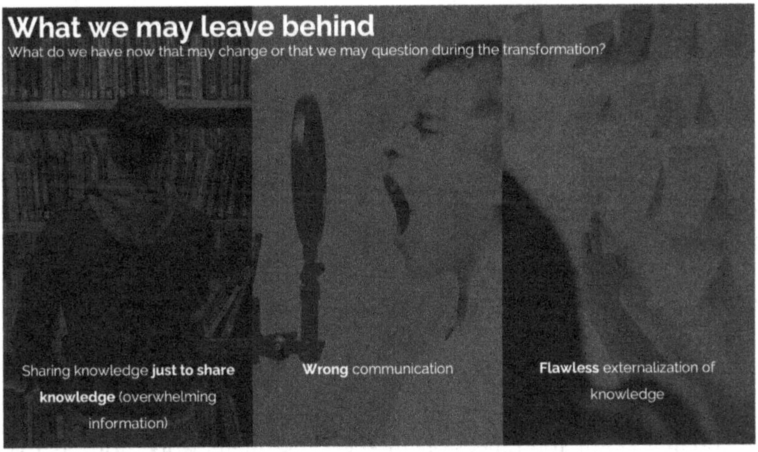
What we may leave behind
What do we have now that may change or that we may question during the transformation?
Sharing knowledge **just to share knowledge** (overwhelming information)
Wrong communication
Flawless externalization of knowledge

Figure 4.2 Nestlé's storyworld – what we can leave behind.
Source: Our own elaboration; images from Unsplash.com.

blocking people and hindering inspiration and collaboration within the team.

- *Flawless externalization of knowledge.* People often link quantity to quality. Talking flawlessly is not always necessary and might cause entropy in communication, hiding what is important from what is not (Figure 4.2).

1.2.2 The storymaking journey

Nestlé participants used the storymaker card set to write their individual transformation stories. Based on the brief, participants designed their prospective stories of transformation to make sense of how they could be recognized as innovative leaders and make innovation happen.

1.3 Results – what happened?

1.3.1 How does change come true?

Participants each set themselves a long-term objective, defining how they would need to change to respond to the organizational needs. Through a series of four workshops, they worked on making this transformation come true, reflecting on the organizational situation, and

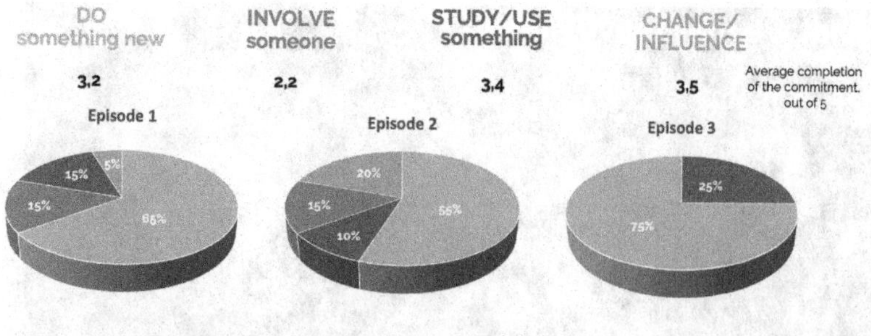

Figure 4.3 Commitments across the episodes.
Source: Our own elaboration.

making one small specific commitment to action that would provide the starting point for reflection in the subsequent workshop, as explained in Chapter 3.

Considering the commitments, on average, those focused on doing something new tended to be more fulfilled. Involving someone seems to bring greater obstacles, while the commitment to invest time in learning and developing professional skills through training was pursued across the episodes (Figure 4.3).

In addition to identifying their long-term objectives, participants were asked to reflect on the main obstacles they expected to face and some items or people who might prove helpful on their journey as *companions* sharing their burden, or as *mentors* providing guidance (see Chapter 3).

We found that participants highlighted different obstacles over the episodes. The first episode saw a relative balance among external obstacles (39%), personal obstacles (33%), and both (28%). The second and third episodes saw a growth in external obstacles (53% and 58%). However, this might correlate with the global pandemic that peaked in many countries involved in the second and third episodes.

Interestingly, 95% of participants picked at least a companion, 50% a colleague, and 75% added someone else in the subsequent episodes. Almost all participants perceived that transformation was more easily achieved with someone else.

Similarly, 80% of participants picked a mentor, a percentage that remained quite stable over the episodes, indicating the likelihood of having a mentor in their professional life.

Finally, 90% of participants picked at least one tool of which 55% opted for a digital tool (55%), and the remainder for physical analog tools.

1.4 What do your stories tell us?

Every participant wrote a narrative to reflect on their individual transformation. To highlight the main value of their stories, they were asked to identify three principles reflecting the most salient points. These principles sum up the driving forces behind the change, while the longer stories represent *how* the transformation is achieved (see Chapter 3).

In the first episode, very different principles emerged related to the specific challenges in this organization, since participants were asked to think about how to work on themselves to be perceived as innovative leaders, without giving them a specific direction. However, over the episodes, they tended to converge more, showing that people influence each other. Overall, the principles that emerged most often were *courage, passion,* and *learning.* Considering the three episodes longitudinally, they seem to suggest three steps to be recognized as innovative leaders:

1 Inspiring others, showing the active role of innovative leaders.
2 Being effective, innovative leaders need to empower others.
3 Changing together and empower others…letting things go.

Interesting to note is that in their stories, the concept of people was particularly relevant, coherently with the challenge of understanding how they can be recognized as innovative leaders. In this case, the initial stories were very abstract, talking about the concept of innovation, the role of people, and the willingness to change. However, in the last episode, the focus shifted to teams collaborating on shared projects.

Figure 4.4 shows the word-clouds of the most frequent principles and words emerging in the stories (see Chapter 5 for further explanations). The great heterogeneity of principles, as well as the large number of words emerging in the word-cloud of the first episode, also indicates the movement of participants over time. People tended to cluster in the second and third episodes, while in the first they were rather sparse. The first two episodes focused on more general words, and the third on more concrete and project-related words (project, development, activity, and commitment).

Through problematizing their transformation, participants understood what it meant to be innovative leaders, then moved toward searching for plans and collaborations to make it happen (Figure 4.5).

Figure 4.4 Individual principles and topics emerging from the stories.
Source: Our own elaboration.

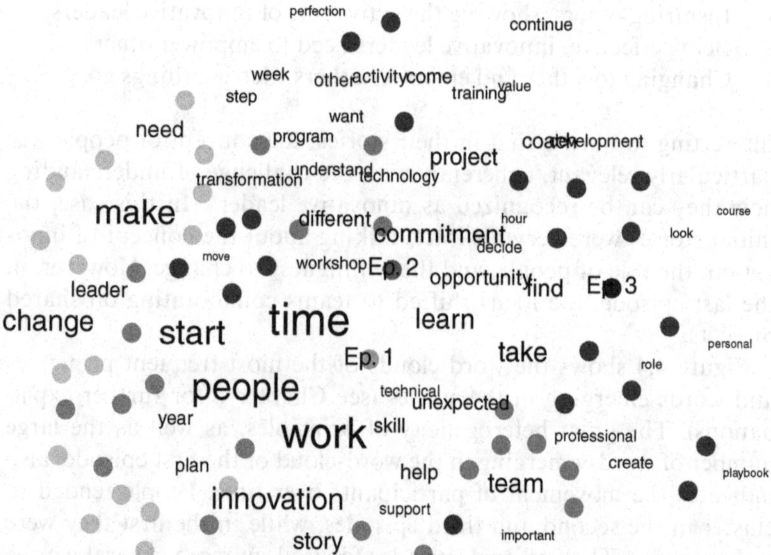

Figure 4.5 The evolution of stories.
Source: Our own elaboration.

1.5 Findings: how did transformation happen?

Organizational transformation requires all members to collectively engage in achieving the new objectives. Hence, we tracked the evolution of individual engagement in the transformation project (see Chapter 3). The engagement path that emerged in these workshops is extremely interesting. The initial engagement was one of the highest values recorded in the storymaking experience by the research team over the years. The average value is around 4.5 out of 5. In this sense, two key variables need to be considered. On the one hand, participants mainly work in innovation activities and workshops, thus very keen on working on these topics. On the other hand, this is probably the most personal challenge among those proposed in the research platform.

Therefore, our storymaking experience faced an even greater challenge: keeping people engaged who started with an already high level of engagement. Indeed, the data show that this experience not only engaged people initially, but kept them constantly engaged over time.

Further, we analyzed how each participant perceived their own story, and whether they found it reasonable and relevant to pursue the transformation path outlined. The perception of meaningfulness followed a similar path to engagement, remaining constant and relatively high throughout the episodes. Each time they faced a new obstacle, hurdle, or opportunity, they had the chance to make sense of it in their stories and keep meaningfulness high (Figure 4.6).

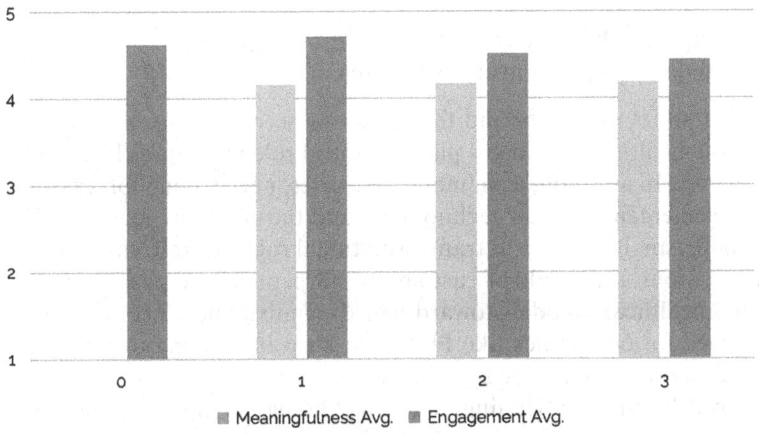

Figure 4.6 Engagement and meaningfulness.

Source: Our own elaboration.

1.6 Conclusion and final reflections

The project that the research team and Nestlé implemented proposed a personal challenge within the organization: 20 participants took concrete action to understand how to effectively be recognized as innovative leaders.

This case shows the potentialities of the storymaking experience to make transformation happen, take an even broader direction (as innovative leaders), and foster individual change.

One participant commented, "I liked the interval length and the personal interactions. These always gave me a checkpoint and an opportunity to articulate what I had actually done". Moreover, the storymaking tools were appreciated as an interactive tool in each step, "Storymaking is indeed a great tool to make plans and visualize where we want to go".

This impacted the flow of the process (as seen in the heterogeneity of principles at the beginning), confirming the power of going through this kind of transformation with a group of colleagues. This also emerged in the comments received at the end of the program, "I appreciated the interactions with others to receive criticism and also to share their thoughts", "I also learnt the importance of listening to other people's stories".

They worked together on their personal transformation, influenced each other, and helped others be critical to make transformation happen.

2 Philips: guiding the transition toward designing modular and configurable solutions

Recent shifts in society and the economic scenario have highlighted that the healthcare industry plays a central role in people's lives more than ever. In addition, as in many industries, new driving forces, such as the emergence of new technologies and the circular economy, play an increasingly important transformational role. Overall, shifts in the expectations and needs of customers and patients are pushing traditional healthcare models toward new disruptive ones. All this drives the need for companies like Philips to keep innovating to make the world healthier and more sustainable.

Royal Philips is a leading health technology company focused on improving people's health and enabling better outcomes across the health continuum from healthy living and prevention to diagnosis, treatment, and home care. Philips leverages advanced technologies and deep clinical and consumer insights to deliver integrated solutions. Headquartered in the Netherlands, the company is a leader in diagnostic imaging, image-guided therapy, patient monitoring, and health informatics, as well as in consumer health and home care. In 2019, Philips generated sales of €19.5 billion with approximately 80,000 employees, offering sales and services in more than 100 countries.

Among the different functions of this multinational, Philips Experience Design focuses on applying design-based research and innovation programs collaborating with other functions, business, and market organizations throughout the firm. Philips Experience Design applies a co-creation approach to innovation, involving users from the very beginning of the innovation process.

This open approach to innovation allows creating solutions that touch millions of lives every day through a workforce of over 500 people from over 35 different countries, and offices located all over the globe in 12 locations.

Philips Experience Design addresses all kinds of healthcare problems and believes that value lies in understanding people's needs, aspirations, and diversity, enabled by design. In other words, good experiences are crucial contributors to good outcomes. A pioneer in applying human-centric design, Philips Designers have historically sought to engage with users and stakeholders to contribute to the creation of its products, services, and applications.

2.1 The challenge

Philips aimed to help people in the organization embrace their personal transformation toward the transition the company has been driving over the past years: from being a product company to a solution company. Through this transition, the organization is strengthening its ability to establish long-term relationships with a broad set of customers and all the different stakeholders in an ecosystem of people, products, and services.

This is in line with the evolving needs and expectations of customers and patients in the health industry and is a great opportunity for Philips. Nonetheless, this requires profound changes in how different teams and functions in the organization work. Philips Experience Design has a unique and strategic position in the organization to support the entire transformation because as designers they strive for end-to-end and bigger-picture thinking, and collaborate with the multiple teams that need to work together. Making this transition happen requires a tremendous shift toward designing modular and configurable solutions across the businesses, acting and thinking differently, and developing new capabilities so as to establish compelling dialogue and collaboration with their business counterparts.

The research aims to engage employees to embrace and make the next step in this change happen. Why not apply the storymaking experience to this challenging setting? Participants write and live their personal stories of transformation to foster the design of modular and configurable solutions. Going through the experience allows dedicating time to framing their purpose within the overall direction and taking action in their daily lives to ensure the transformation comes true. Therefore, 20 participants, mostly with a design-oriented background, and from different studios around the world, were involved in the project, acting as catalysts of the initiative so as to unlock more conscious growth toward new meaningful paths.

2.2 The storymaker workshop

2.2.1 Setting the storyworld

The Philips and research core teams worked together to craft the storyworld for this transformation journey and found a way to challenge those who wanted to join the research quest and set the boundaries of the stories they wrote.

The Brief: As Philips continues its transition toward a solutions company, Philips Experience Design continues to play an important role. Not only is experience a core element of the quadruple aim, but the holistic approach and user-focus are naturally compatible with delivering integrated care along end-to-end pathways. As designers, they are comfortable with balancing different stakeholder needs, making ideas tangible, and navigating through ambiguity until reaching clear and common goals that help improve the lives of customers and users.

The transition is a tremendous opportunity for Experience Design to support business in better addressing the user and customer needs on a solution level, instead of focusing mainly on the touchpoint level.

However, the move to cross-business solutions created challenges on roles and responsibilities. Moreover, the designers' broad skills, deep knowledge, and expertise are not always recognized by their counterparts in the business. Furthermore, from a solutions point of view, the Philips portfolio sometimes has overlaps and inconsistencies, with clear opportunities for improving the user experience. And this is exactly where Philips Experience Design can make a difference and add value.

Thus, the need to move toward a situation where the Experience Design role in solution creation is easily understood with clear evidence of the value brought to customers, end users, and the organization. Therefore, the research challenge brief was formulated as follows: *How can we, as Philips Experience Design, foster the transition toward design for modular and configurable solutions?*

The Pillars: The Philips leadership and research teams jointly identified three fundamental elements that define the boundaries of the direction that Philips foresees. These are the strategic pillars aimed at achieving modularity and configurability to identify what the future world would be and what to leave behind, thus pivotal in crafting the participants' stories:

- *Open access to assets and documentation:* Fostering an environment where people's work can be easily found by everyone else in the organization. If this does not happen, too much time is spent in defining things from scratch, dissipating time and energy, and losing momentum for synergy and acceleration.
- *Repair, repurpose, and reuse over reinvent.* The second pillar aims to limit the production of waste during teamwork, both from a financial but mostly a sustainability perspective. People need the ability to look at what is at their disposal and develop it so as to give it a new life within the ecosystem.
- *Maintain and evolve collaboratively.* The third and final pillar is a crucial enabler of the previous two. Instead of having centralized teams responsible for the development of specific solutions, they need to leverage the power of the Philips community and ensure that everyone actively contributes to what already exists (Figure 4.7).

What can be left behind: The Philips and research core team jointly defined a set of elements characterizing the current setting in which Philips operates that need to be overcome in the transformation journey so as to enable people to activate the change:

- *The siloed creation of our assets and documentation.* Collaboration and innovation are empowered by the opportunity of having the right resources at the right time, enabling thinking as a horizontal community rather than vertical silos.
- *Tools and platforms that do not allow us to find each other's work easily and contribute to each other's work.* Following the previous point, to truly tap into the Philips global community potential,

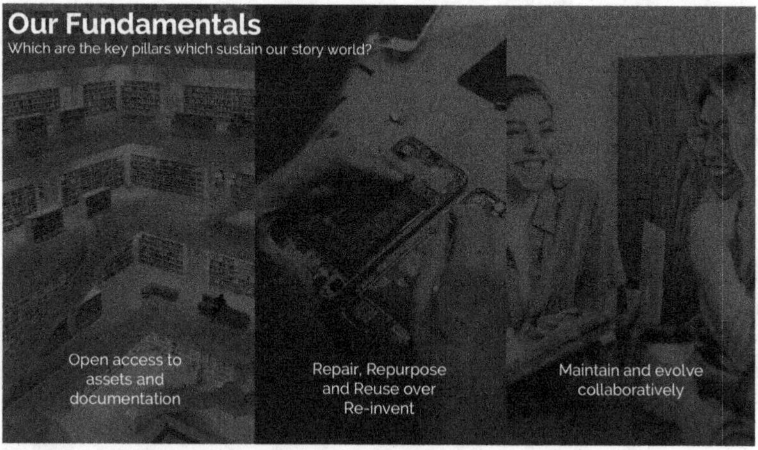

Figure 4.7 Philips' storyworld: our fundamentals.
Source: Our own elaboration; images from Unsplash.com.

tools and platforms should be leveraged to establish new connections and meaningful relationships. Therefore, inertia and rigidity in using tools and working instruments should be avoided.

- *Being seen as a supplier to the business rather than a strategic partner.* The transition toward the new horizon also brings critical shifts in the way in which relationships with internal stakeholders are managed. Rather than a mere business supplier, Philips Design aims to further improve its position as a strategic partner, teaming up with internal stakeholders along their own journey with their customers in the pursuit of continuous improvement (Figure 4.8).

2.2.2 The storymaking journey

As in the other organizations, Philips' participants used the storymaker card set to write their individual transformation stories. Based on the challenge proposed, participants designed their prospective stories of transformation to make sense of the change and understand how Philips Experience Design could foster the transition toward designing modular and configurable solutions.

Before presenting the results, important to note is that while the other research partner companies embarked on a digital experience as a result of COVID-19 restrictions, the Philips project was always intended to take place in a digital mode to fully embrace the intrinsic

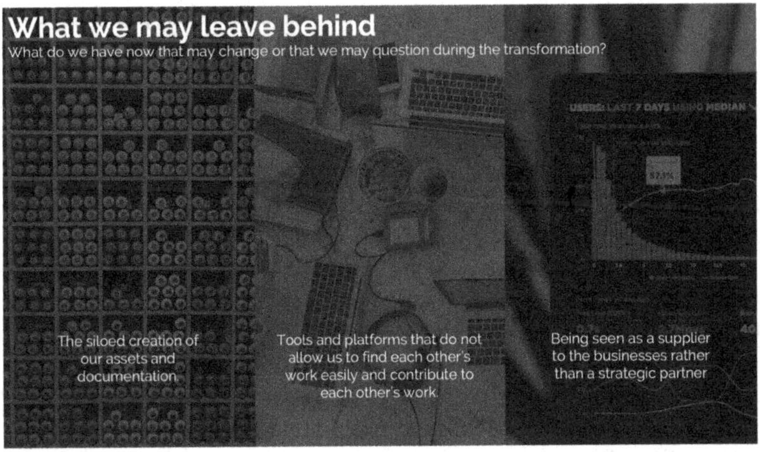

Figure 4.8 Philips' storyworld: what we can leave behind.
Source: Our own elaboration; images from Unsplash.com.

nature of the challenge posed. Therefore, 20 participants from the Philips Experience Design community from different studios around the globe, including India, Israel, Europe, and the United States, voluntarily took part in the project and the storymaking journey.

2.3 *Results – what happened?*

2.3.1 How does change come true?

Over the episodes, the use of the story-coach card set led to different insights regarding the participants' transformation journey. First, participants faced different obstacles in pursuing their desired change, including a lack of competencies or individual hurdles in facing the change, and finding the time to dedicate to their personal transformation.

Organizational resistance, such as differences in stakeholder needs, was classified as external obstacles. Finally, the hurdles related to the two categories were clustered into a separate category.

Interestingly, the presence of external obstacles was highly relevant and quite stable across the first (58%), second (64%), and third (58%) episodes. Personal and mixed obstacles though were perfectly balanced during the first and third episodes (21%), while episode 2 saw a slight decrease in the mixed obstacles (21% personal obstacles and 15% mixed obstacles).

The use of the *Companion* and *Mentor* cards instead provided evidence of the cohesion of people in the Philips Experience Design community. In fact, 100% of participants picked at least one companion, while 73% added more than one colleague in the subsequent episodes. Transformation is a shared process, and participants felt the need for mutual support and trust. Similarly, 73% of participants picked a mentor, highlighting the need for guidance in keeping the overall vision stable or support in pursuing individual commitments.

The design-oriented nature of the community also brought a sense of pragmatism in the use of *Objects*. In total, 95% of participants picked at least one tool of which 32% were digital and 32% were analog. In addition, 18% picked an abstract tool as a spirit guide and informal communication, while 18% preferred to rely on their technical skills by choosing software as a working instrument (Figure 4.9).

Regarding their commitments, on average, participants tended to commit most to concrete actions to actualize their transformation path. For instance, participants activated themselves in promoting new initiatives to scale solutions at the global level, or new activities put in place to push the boundaries of what they were used to doing. Involving someone in the change, studying/learning, and changing/influencing someone were less pursued along the path. Moreover, among the different categories of commitments, those easily embraced were *do things differently*, *involve someone in the change*, and *study and learn something.* While *changing or influencing others* seemed to face greater obstacles.

2.4 What do your stories tell us?

Different principles were defined over the episodes, setting the tone of voice of the collective stories. In the first episode, *collaboration* and

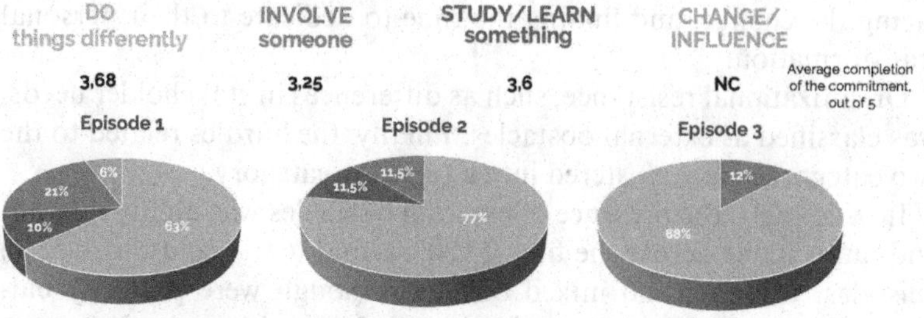

Figure 4.9 Commitments over the episodes.
Source: Our own elaboration.

change emerged as key values, highlighting the need to establish peer-to-peer relationships within the organization to make the transformation happen. The new concepts that emerged in the second episode were *inspire, trust*, and *methodology*. Other emerging principles instead suggest the importance of factuality in the change: *make, dare, lead*. Finally, the third episode confirmed a deeper sense of activation with keywords such as *daring, action*, and *working*. Moreover, *fluidity, continuous, agile,* and *iterative* indicate the way the transformation should happen.

The stories written by participants followed an intriguing path. In the first episode, most stories related to the role of experience, anchored in broad organizational topics and supported by words like *solution, organization, experience,* and *transform*. Stories in the second episode instead mostly revolved around the need to *change* and *work* as a *team*. Here, linked to the emerging transformation concept, the role of the *commitment* also started to take hold. Finally, in the third episode, the content of the stories was very straightforward, as most participants discussed the role of *commitment* to *making change happen*. Interestingly, the three steps highlight an evolution in the way they approached their transformation. Focused at the beginning on delving into the organizational needs to be addressed to make the change come true, over the episodes, the stories became more human, leading participants to determine their own personal commitment within the overall direction.

This emerged more clearly in the additional analysis (Figure 4.10) of the words participants used in their stories across the different episodes. Interesting to note is that in articulating previously mentioned concepts, they moved coherently across different clusters of words: finding cohesion at the beginning in the blue cluster, enlarging in the

Figure 4.10 Individual principles and topics emerging from the stories.
Source: Our own elaboration.

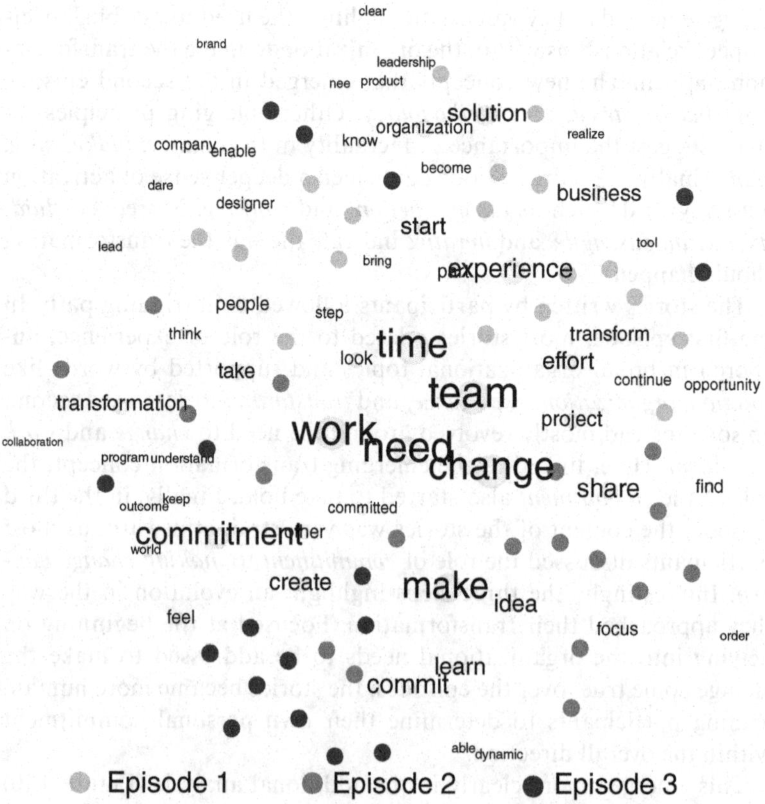

Figure 4.11 The evolution of the stories.
Source: Our own elaboration.

grey cluster, and finally, converging again in the orange cluster. This visualization shows how participants collectively transformed in approaching the transition toward the design of modular and configurable solutions, advancing their own story, but at the same time keeping pace with others (Figure 4.11).

2.5 Findings – how did transformation happen?

As a final step, we analyzed the data in terms of the level of engagement and meaningfulness over the three episodes. The findings show what transforming toward an innovative direction really means. The Philips participants are an active and thoughtful community, able to dive deep into the experience with a curious mindset. In fact, their level of engagement was very high, with an average value of 4. This highlights not only the great interest they showed, but also the effectiveness of the *storymaking experience* in keeping people engaged over time.

In addition, worth noting is that the high level of engagement was supported by the growth in meaningfulness over time. Delving into the experience by making sense of the change and acting concretely toward it, participants found that what they were writing in their stories became more meaningful. This suggests that driving actions and accountability are crucial for making transformation more meaningful to people engaged in the process. At the same time, this perception nurtures engagement, keeping people focused on small significant steps over time (Figure 4.12).

2.6 *Conclusion and final reflections*

The project jointly developed by the research team and Philips triggered a transformation toward a new organizational challenge: about 20 participants activated themselves by taking concrete actions to foster the design of modular and configurable solutions. Moreover, the participants from all around the globe established new meaningful connections by sharing their perspectives and enhancing each other's stories.

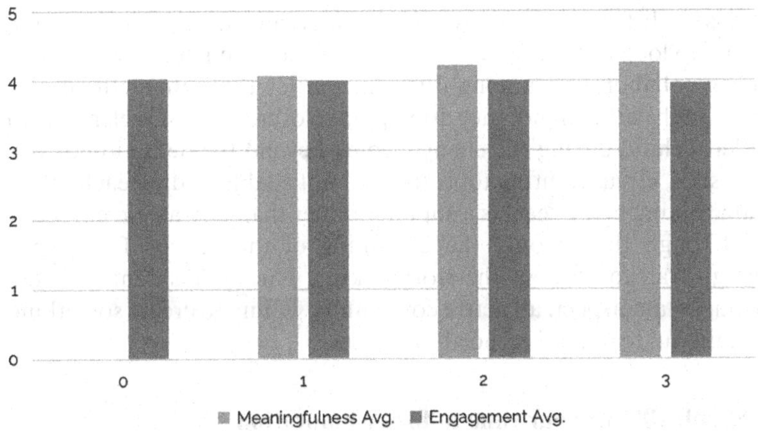

Figure 4.12 Engagement and meaningfulness.
Source: Our own elaboration.

This project clearly shows that transformation requires not only that people understand the overall direction, but making it personal by articulating and actualizing it. Hence, two layers are closely intertwined in this process: on the one hand, the sensemaking activity is needed to find meaning throughout the transformation, and on the other hand, people engage in taking small concrete actions to make it happen.

Nevertheless, this is not solely an individual path, as only a collaborative effort can establish new synergies among the stories and make transformation happen. In particular, multiple concrete actions were taken by participants to embrace the change. Some successfully engaged key stakeholders or team members through presenting new initiatives to make the new organizational scenario a reality. Others decided to work on their own identity, trying to acquire new skills that would enable change: business-related tools to integrate a more design-oriented background with the company's needs, or new technical skills to become more effective in communicating the new strategic direction. Finally, others focused either on the design or the search for new or existing tools within the organization that would enable them to share, organize, and transfer the design perspective to different actors, including slides for a new proposal to be pitched, experiential tools, or digital platforms.

The collective efforts to activate change within the organization are significantly linked to the storyworld from which it all began. The collection of actions is a sum of small steps performed by the Philips Experience Design community toward reaching modularity and configurability. On the one hand, they brought concreteness to the strategic pillars identified at the beginning of the project: promoting open access to different resources within the organization, enhancing the ability to look at what is at their disposal and giving it a new life, nurturing collaboration among different parties throughout the evolution. On the other hand, they attempted to overcome some elements to be left behind during the change: going beyond the definition of vertical silos, circumventing tools that did not enable finding each other, and avoiding being seen as a supplier rather than a strategic partner.

Although this is only the beginning of the Philips Experience Design transformation, the storymaking journey has demonstrated an important aspect: an active community willing to create something meaningful together is crucial for success.

3 Sasol: 10% of your time to foster innovation

The chemical industry is a mature sector assuring high returns and margins for decades. Today, as with many major industries, it is being challenged by new competitive forces and megatrends, such as digitalization, climate change, and increased attention to sustainability. Therefore, chemical companies feel the need to foster innovation as never before.

Sasol is an international integrated chemicals and energy company headquartered in Johannesburg, South Africa. Sasol was established in 1950 and built on the Fischer–Tropsch process developed by German chemists and engineers in the early 1900s known as coal liquefaction. Today, the company develops and commercializes technologies, operating global-scale facilities to produce a range of high-value product streams, including liquid fuels, chemicals, and low-carbon electricity. The company is listed on the JSE in South Africa and the New York Stock Exchange and has more than 30,000 employees with operations in 31 countries.

Sasol's chemicals business includes the production, marketing, and sales of chemical products both in Southern Africa and internationally, selling to key markets such as fabric and home care, health and personal care, energy and natural resources, automotive, agriculture, construction, manufacturing, and packaging. The chemicals business is divided into two niche groups, namely, base chemicals that include fertilizers, polymers, and solvents, and performance chemicals, comprising key products including surfactants, surfactant intermediates, fatty alcohols, linear alkyl benzene (LAB), short-chain linear alpha olefins, ethylene, mineral oil-based and synthetic paraffin waxes, cresylic acids, high-quality carbon solutions, and high-purity and ultra-high-purity alumina.

By combining the talent of people and technological advantages, Sasol's chemicals business has been a pioneer in innovation for over six decades. In recent years, the company's stated ambition is to transition toward a more specialty chemicals portfolio, propelling its leadership to foster an innovation culture that led to the creation of a dedicated growth and innovation team to drive initiatives that leverage the best practices, tools, and techniques from both internal and external ecosystems.

3.1 The challenge

One of the initiatives that the growth and innovation team proposed was encouraging employees to dedicate 10% of their work time to fostering innovation. Many tech companies have successfully promoted self-reflection and creative thinking to keep innovation happening. The clear message to employees is: innovation is part of your job, no matter your job title or function. Still, as often happens, fostering innovation to change people's habits is not easy. The research aim is to engage people to make innovation happen. Why not use the storycoach to help people embrace this initiative of using 10% of their time to foster innovation?

Relying on the storymaking experience, participants designed a personal story to bring them to use 10% of their time to foster innovation, thinking about ways, people, and moments that would allow changing their daily routine. Twenty participants were involved in the project to change and embrace this initiative and start to consider innovation as a daily mission.

3.2 The storymaker workshop

3.2.1 Setting the storyworld

The Sasol and research core teams worked together to craft the storyworld for this transformation journey and found a way to challenge those who wanted to join the research quest and set the boundaries of the stories they wrote.

The Brief: We foresee a future world with an increasing focus on sustainability and growing population, urbanization, digitalization, and mobility. We have an excellent business and talented people, and we see opportunities in this future world where we can make lives better through the application of our innovative mindset. You have the opportunity to use 10% of your time to grow your innovation mindset. Hence: *What is your personal commitment to use this 10%?*

The Pillars: The Sasol leadership and research teams jointly identified three fundamental elements that Sasol embodies today, deemed pivotal to the transformation journey and in crafting the participants' stories:

- *Our ways of working: We care, we innovate, we deliver.* The first pillar highlights Sasol's fundamental elements, caring about all stakeholders, the tendency to foster innovation, and execute projects.
- *Sasol's aspirational culture and values.* The second pillar reminds participants of the organizational culture and values that need to be a guiding light in this transformation journey.
- *We continue to work with the seven fields of action to support our growth and innovation ambitions.* The third and final pillar links this project with the existing change mechanisms and innovation projects that the company is already undertaking (customer centricity, higher purpose and performance, etc.; Figure 4.13).

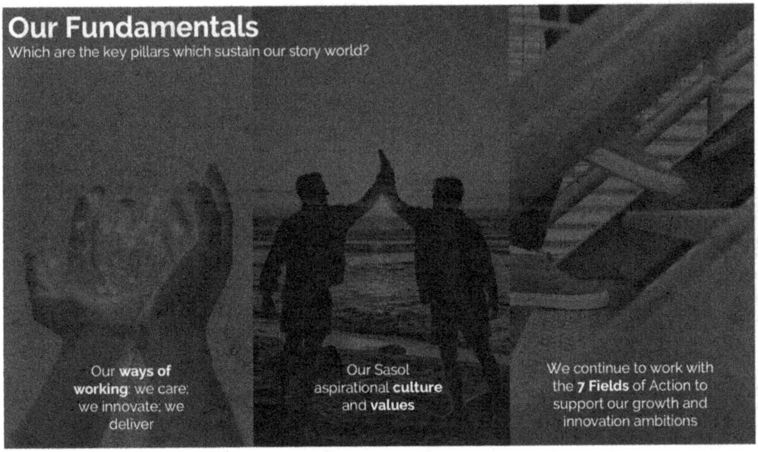

Figure 4.13 Sasol's storyworld: our fundamentals.
Source: Our own elaboration; images from Unsplash.com.

What can be left behind: Finally, the Sasol and the research core teams jointly defined areas to consider along this change journey that could be left behind, but phrased positively to express what was expected from the transformation:

- *Collaborate and innovate. Don't think that only "experts" are responsible for innovation.* People in any organization may think they are not entitled to innovation; this mistaken belief should be left behind. Anyone can and should collaborate and innovate.
- *Speak Up. Your view matters.* Following the previous point, people might be afraid of talking about something they feel they do not own; this is not the case. Anyone can and should speak up and share her/his view on innovation.
- *Be bold, be agile. Don't be scared of failure.* Many people are afraid of failure, but innovation is not a straightforward process, failure is part of the game. Dare to try.
- *Don't use the 10% on what you do anyway.* The challenge is to use this time to think about things that wouldn't happen anywhere else creatively, so don't use it for what should stay in the remaining 90% (Figure 4.14).

3.2.2 The storymaking journey

Sasol participants used the storymaker card set to write their individual transformation stories. Based on the brief, participants would design

Figure 4.14 Sasol's storyworld: what we can leave behind, but stated in such a way as to indicate the desired outcome.

Source: Our own elaboration; images from Unsplash.com.

their prospective stories of transformation to make sense of change and understand how to use 10% of their time to foster innovation.

To note prior to presenting the results is that Sasol was to be the first research partner to use the story-coach and physically kicked off the program on February 21, 2020 in Hamburg, the same day COVID-19 appeared in Italy. The subsequent episodes took place digitally as initially planned. Therefore, Sasol is the only partner that experienced the physical version of the workshop to create episode 1.

3.3 Results – what happened?

3.3.1 How does change come true?

Participants set themselves a long-term objective, defining how they would need to change to respond to the organizational need. Throughout the four workshops, everyone worked on making this transformation come true, reflecting on the organizational situation, and making one small specific commitment to action that would provide the starting point for reflection in the subsequent workshop as explained in Chapter 3. Regarding the commitments, on average, personal commitments focused on doing or improving something tended to be more fulfilled, while having an impact or involving someone else faced greater obstacles.

In addition to identifying their long-term objectives, participants were asked to reflect on the main obstacles they expected to face and some items or people who might prove helpful on their journey as *companions* sharing their burden, or as *mentors* providing guidance (see also Chapter 3).

We found that participants highlighted different obstacles over the episodes. The first episode saw a good balance among external (48%) and personal obstacles (48%), with some (4%) highlighting both types. The second episode saw a shift toward personal obstacles (53%), and remained stable in the other two clusters (37% external, and 10% both), returning to a more balanced situation in the third (47% external, 43% personal, and 10% both). Generally, participants tended to perceive both personal (individual) and external obstacles even though in the second episode, the COVID emergency that participants started experiencing had a considerable impact first on the personal and then on the external dimensions.

Interestingly, 95% of participants picked at least one companion, half chose a colleague, and 75% added someone else in the subsequent episodes. Transformation is not a simple process; participants felt the need for more companions to face the change.

Similarly, 79% of participants picked a mentor, highlighting the need for experienced support in the transformation journey.

In total, 84% of participants picked at least one tool, mainly focusing on digital tools (65%). Interestingly, 18% highlighted the human dimension of *relationships* among the tools or skills (12%). 5% highlighted collective activities as a tool, such as workshops.

3.4 What do your stories tell us?

Every participant wrote a narrative to reflect on their individual transformation, highlighting the main value of their story, and identifying three principles reflecting the salient points. These principles sum up the driving forces behind the change, while the longer stories represent *how* the transformation was achieved (see Chapter 3).

In the first episode, the emerging principle *change* remained stable throughout the episodes. In the beginning, there was greater heterogeneity among the words, while in the end, the common words remained, showing that participants converged (and influenced each other) over time.

With regard to their stories, interesting to note is that at the beginning, there was good alignment between the principles and the content of the stories, with *change* emerging again. The tone of voice in the first episode was rather inspirational, showing the role of helping people understand where they want to go with the transformation journey. Across the episodes, a broader and more heterogeneous set of words emerged. A joint reading of the principles and stories shows something peculiar: participants were going in the same direction, but in different ways. Moreover, a gradual movement from aspirational words (*change, need*) to more concrete ones (*work, get, time, make, collaboration, project, etc.*) emerged moving along the episodes. In other words, the transformation was happening.

Figure 4.15 shows the word-clouds of the most used principles and words in the stories (see Chapter 5 for further explanations). The stories written followed an interesting path. In the first episode, *problem* emerged as a central world, highlighting the first episode's interpretation role. This was supported by other words such as *new* or *problem.* The second episode allowed transitioning to the third, and again we saw a strong shift toward concrete concepts such as *meeting, project, make, commit,* and *plan.* Completing the previous analysis, we looked at how the words changed as participants moved across the different episodes. Figure 4.16 shows this analysis and that it is not merely a

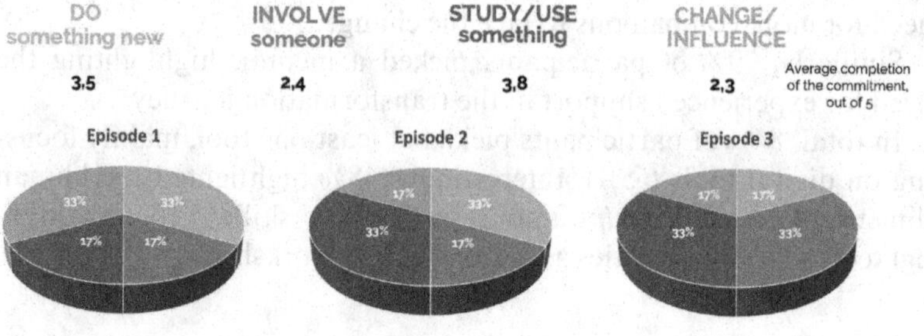

Figure 4.15 Commitments across the episodes.
Source: Our own elaboration.

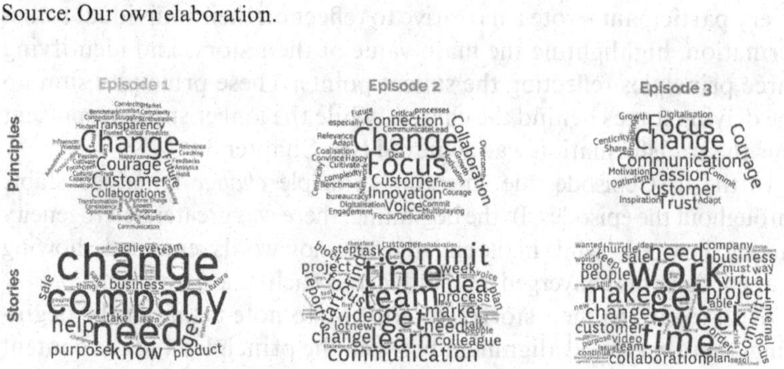

Figure 4.16 Individual principles and topics emerging from the stories.
Source: Our own elaboration.

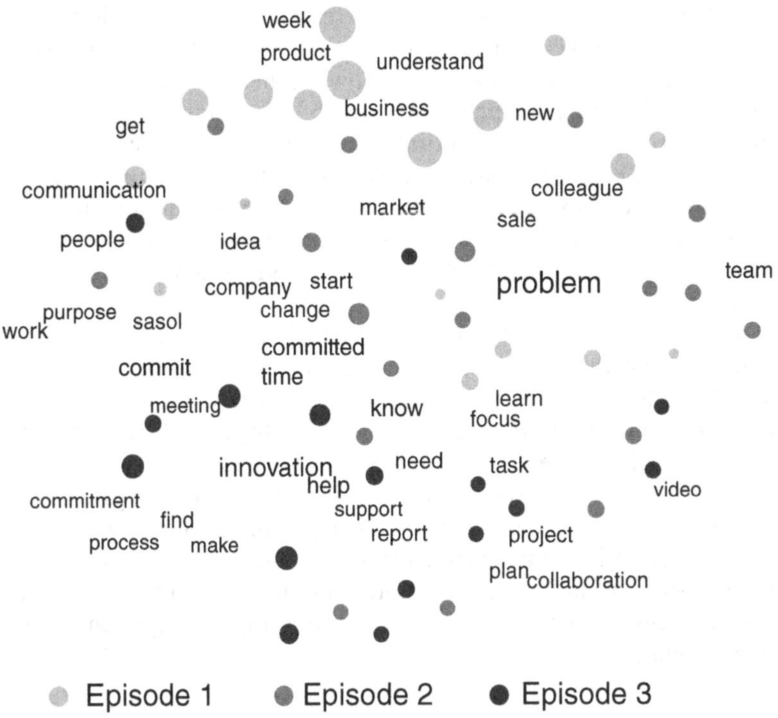

Figure 4.17 The evolution of the stories.
Source: Our own elaboration.

matter of the concepts used on average, but also how participants moved together across different clusters of words: from the words in the blue cluster to the words in the orange clusters. This means that by transforming individually, they also transformed as a collective. Thus, the transformation process they embraced triggered the innovation process. They problematized their transformation to understand what using 10% of their time for growth and innovation meant to each participant (Figure 4.17).

3.5 Findings – how did transformation happen?

Organizational transformation requires all members to engage in collectively achieving the new objectives. Hence, we tracked the evolution of individual engagement in the transformation project (-see Chapter 3 on measurement). The engagement path that emerged in these workshops is extremely interesting and shows what it really means to make innovation happen. The starting point was very good with an average value of 4, showing the great interest of participants. As often happens, the idea of doing innovation can be much more engaging than actually innovating. Indeed, engagement at the end of episode 1 – when participants made their first commitment to make innovation happen – was lower. Still, the storymaking experience shows its effectiveness in the subsequent episode with growing engagement in the original value even when "innovation is happening".

Further, we analyzed how each participant perceived their own story, and whether they found it both reasonable and relevant to pursue the outlined transformation path. The growth in engagement over time is supported by the perceived meaningfulness of what participants are doing. Indeed, over time, we see the increasing meaningfulness of the stories. Through this transformation journey, every time they faced a new obstacle, hurdle, or opportunity, they were able to make sense of it in their story. In proceeding through the episodes, their stories gradually became more and more meaningful to them. This perception of meaningfulness nurtured their engagement in the transformation (Figure 4.18).

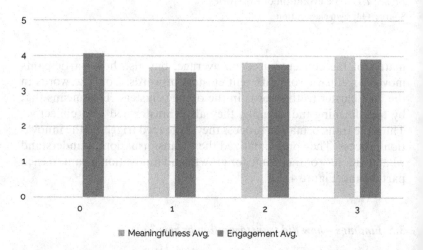

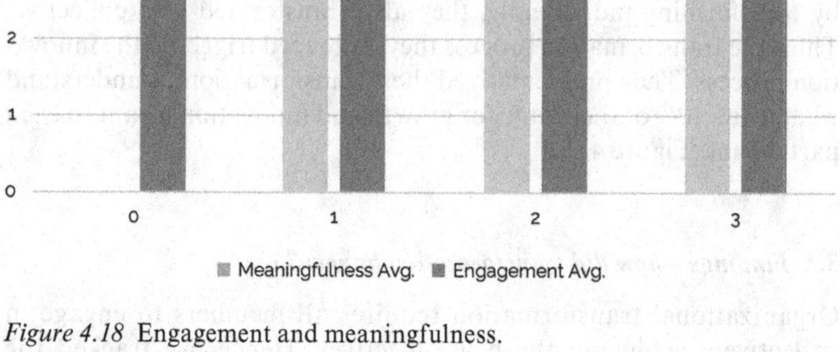

Figure 4.18 Engagement and meaningfulness.
Source: Our own elaboration.

3.6 Conclusion and final reflections

The project that the research team and Sasol implemented sparked commitment throughout the organization: 20 employees took concrete action to understand how to use 10% of their time to foster innovation.

This project clearly shows that innovation calls for a sensemaking process where participants start their transformation, question the meaning of the innovation process, and then take concrete actions to make it happen.

Engaging people in transformation is challenging. The measurement supports this, showing a decrease in engagement when moving from *ideation* to *execution* when participants take action. However, if supported in creating a meaningful path, people will again engage in innovation activities and make them happen.

4 Sintetica: digital transformation in a human-centric organization

Organizations are increasingly facing a radical shift in their internal functioning, with digital technologies disrupting the competitive environment. To succeed in such an ever-changing context, pioneering organizations are proposing ways to weave the opportunities of digitalization into their organizational environment.

Sintetica is a pharmaceutical company established in Switzerland in 1921. It delivers injectable anesthetics and analgesics to patients worldwide, leveraging the strong innovative approach developed over the years. Sintetica employs 300 people in Europe from 29 different countries in the world. The headquarters are in Mendrisio (Switzerland) with sites in Germany, Austria, and the UK.

Over the last few years, the company has been recognized with numerous awards. Among others, Corporate Vision's Small Business Awards went to Sintetica as a pharmaceutical company of the year in Switzerland in 2016, 2017, and 2018. Augusto Mitidieri, the then CEO, was awarded the European CEO of the Year Award in 2016, 2017, and 2018, and the most influential CEO in Europe for 2019. Other awards include Best Pharmaceutical Company in Switzerland at the European Enterprise Awards, European Pharmaceutical CEO Champion at the Business Worldwide CEO Awards, Excellence in HR – Managing Direction and VP Human Resource of the year awards at the Worldwide Business Review, Growth Company Division of the Year (Global Division) at the ACQ5 Awards, and the prestigious Le Fonti Awards.

This incredible list highlights the two main souls of the company: on the one hand, the awards speak to the strong technical leadership, and on the other hand, bright ideas, people management, and governance. In Sintetica, people are at the core, driving performance, fostering creativity, informed risk-taking, and providing an exciting environment. Their ambition is to be a *great place to work*, thus placing emphasis on improving everyday life and environmental sustainability. From a cultural perspective, their strategy translates into a precise strategic concept: a human-centered organization where every individual is considered an innovation leader. Responsibility and merit are at the center and shape the organizational models and behaviors.

Over the past years, the management has worked hard to make the human-centered organization a reality. Today, the company aims to bring this human-centered organization to the next level to understand what digital transformation means for an organization where human beings are at the center.

4.1 The challenge

Sintetica aimed to explore what it means for a human-centered organization to embrace digital transformation. The challenge resides in the willingness to move beyond the idea that digital transformation means replacing people to increase efficiency. The CEO's vision was that digital transformation should facilitate human empowerment and enablement. Therefore, technologies should not be conceived as substitutes for humans, but as enhancers of their capabilities, mindset, and skills.

The research platform is the perfect environment to put this vision into practice. Through the storymaking experience, participants designed a story aimed at identifying what they should change in their daily working life and what they should learn to embrace the opportunities provided by digital technologies, while nonetheless maintaining their role at the center. Twenty-eight participants were involved in this journey: they represented the seeds of the transformation, pursuing two months of research focused on how a human-centered organization can embody the opportunities of a digital transformation.

4.2 The storymaker workshop

4.2.1 Setting the storyworld

The Sintetica and research core teams worked together to craft the storyworld for this individual transformation journey into the digital environment. Together, they found a way to challenge the participants who wanted to join the research quest and set the boundaries of the stories they wrote.

The Brief: We live in a world where digital technologies are increasingly pervasive and offer ever-more opportunities. With the human-centric organization project, Sintetica aimed to always place people at the center. Digital transformation is often confused with replacing people with machines, but this is not what we intend. We want technologies to increase people's capabilities and not destroy or make them obsolete, hence our question: *How do you have to change – and what do you have to learn to do – to take advantage of digital opportunities while remaining at the center?*

The Pillars: The Sintetica leadership and the research teams identified four fundamental points that embody the company today and are pivotal to the transformation journey, and thus in crafting the participants' stories:

- *Everyone is the leader of the transformation.* The first pillar highlights Sintetica's DNA, the need to put humans at the center as leaders in the organization.
- *Everyone is responsible for the change.* The second pillar reminds participants that to be a leader, they need to take responsibility as well as credit.
- *Humans think, they don't succumb.* The third pillar reminds participants that human beings have the ability to think and should be empowered by the digitalization process.
- *Technology enhances, not limits.* The fourth and final pillar is coherent with the CEO's vision that technology is an opportunity for personal growth and learning (Figure 4.19).

What can be left behind: Finally, the Sintetica and research core teams jointly defined a set of points that partly describe today's situation, but may change throughout the transformation journey:

- *Focus on product and process: Services and organizational routines can be subject to innovation.* The first area invites participants to not stick to current processes or products but change them if needed.
- *Function like silos: New skills may be needed that we do not value today.* Building on the previous point, people should move beyond the traditional boundaries of the organization and be open to new competencies and collaborations.

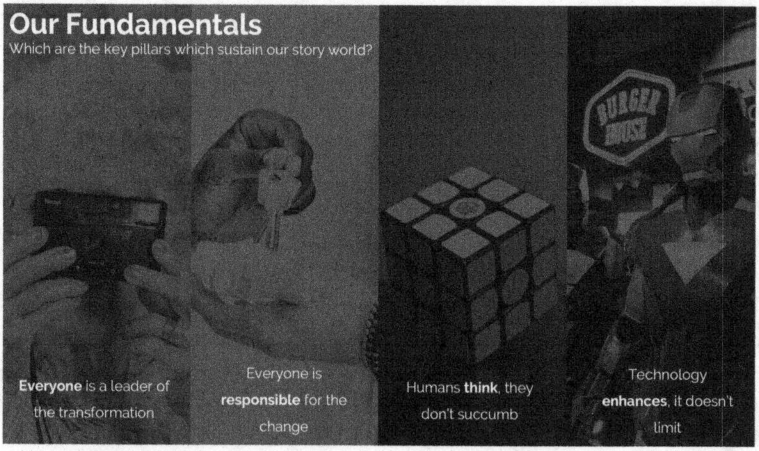

Figure 4.19 Sintetica's storyworld: our fundamentals.
Source: Our own elaboration; images from Unsplash.com.

- *Know-how (knowing how to do it) can leave room for know-where (knowing where to look for it).* In a changing environment, it is much more critical to learn where knowledge resides rather than simply acquiring it.

4.2.2 The storymaking journey

Sintetica's participants used the storymaker card set to write their individual transformation stories. Based on the brief presented, participants designed their prospective stories of transformation to make sense of change and understand how they needed to change to take advantage of the opportunities created by the digital transformation.

4.3 Results – what happened?

4.3.3 How does change come true?

Participants set a long-term objective, defining how they would have to change to respond to the organizational needs. Throughout the four workshops, participants worked on making this transformation come true, reflecting on the organizational situation, and making one specific small commitment to action that would provide the starting point for reflection in the subsequent workshop (see Chapter 3). On average, the personal tendency to focus on doing something new tended

Figure 4.20 Sintetica's storyworld: what we can leave behind.
Source: Our own elaboration; images from Unsplash.com.

to prevail over other types of commitments (Figure 4.20). Further, participants increasingly committed to involving somebody else, implying that transformation journeys cannot be accomplished alone.

In addition to identifying their long-term objectives, participants were asked to reflect on the main obstacles they expected to face, and items or people who might prove helpful on their journey as *companions* sharing their burden, or as *mentors* providing guidance (see Chapter 3).

We found that participants highlighted different obstacles over the episodes. The first episode saw a balance among external (44%) and personal obstacles (51%), with some (5%) highlighting both. The situation remained stable over the subsequent episodes. This means that individuals can overcome their main obstacles: almost half were manageable by the participants themselves, as they did not reside in external factors. Through working on their own capabilities and acquiring new skills or knowledge, individuals can overcome their barriers to change.

Interestingly, 89% of participants picked at least one companion for their journey, and in 58% of cases, the companion was a colleague from Sintetica. In addition, along the journey, 55% of participants perceived the need to add further companions to be successful in their transformation. Similarly, 79% of participants picked a mentor, highlighting the need for experienced support in the transformation journey. The choice of mentor remained unchanged throughout.

Further, 73% of participants picked at least one tool, of which 65% chose digital and the remainder analog tools. Interesting to note is that despite concerning digital transformation, analog tools (such as books) are still relevant to people. It appears that even in the case of change, people rely on what they know and makes them feel safe.

4.4 What do your stories tell us?

Participants wrote a narrative to reflect on their individual transformation, highlighting the main value of their stories, and identifying three principles reflecting their salient points. These principles sum up the driving forces behind the change, while the longer stories indicate *how* the transformation was achieved (see Chapter 3).

In terms of the principles chosen to describe the stories, some fundamental aspects recurred throughout the episodes, namely, *collaboration*, *sharing,* and *trust.* Initially, the principles touched on a broad set of thematic areas (examples include *mindfulness*, *leader*, *growth*, *challenge*, and *change*), while in the second and third episodes, they tended to become much more centered on the relationship concept (examples are *collaboration*, *involvement*, *delegation*, *listening*, and *communication*).

Interestingly, at the beginning, the stories mainly concentrated on change at the company level, but in episodes 2 and 3, they became much more people oriented. More precisely, in episode 2, the work of people to make projects and activities happen appears central, while in episode 3, the concept of *people* was substituted with *team*, therefore relating to the emerging principles of collaboration and relationships.

These findings confirm what had already emerged in relation to commitment: transformation takes place when the action is collaborative and collective.

Completing the analysis, we looked at how the words participants used changed across the different episodes. Figure 4.21 shows the word-clouds of the most used principles and words in the stories (see Chapter 5 for further explanations). The stories written by participants followed an intriguing path: in the first episode, the stories identified the need to dedicate time to working on making digitalization change happen. In the second episode, the need emerged to understand how to make this change happen, as participants identified change projects and reflected on the managerial changes needed to support the transformation, in particular, the organizational aspects.

In the third episode, the stories became even more operational: the same management aspects were discussed, but making transformation happen called for team involvement and commitment to the project.

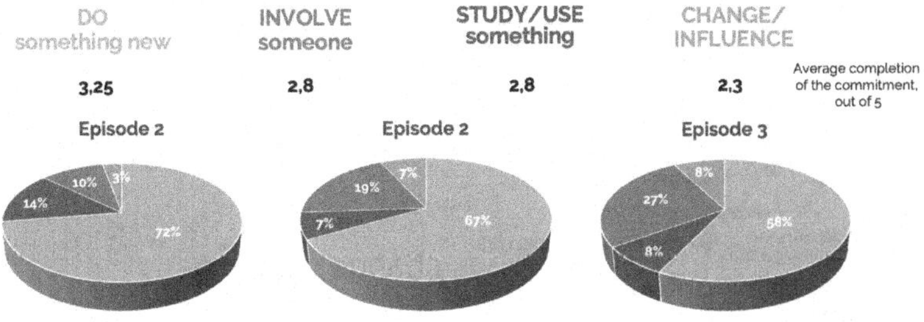

Figure 4.21 Commitments across the episodes.
Source: Our own elaboration.

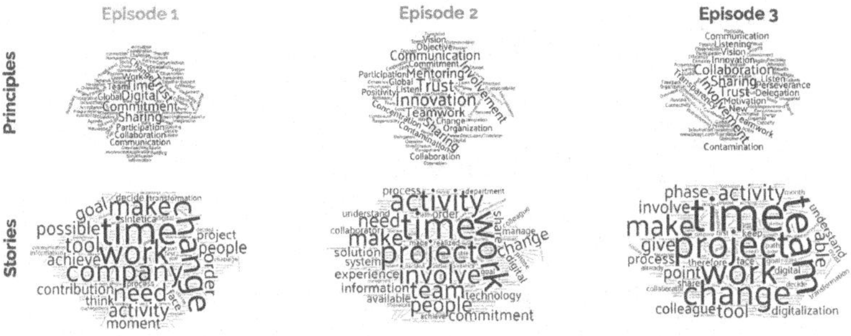

Figure 4.22 Individual principles and topics emerging from the stories.
Source: Our own elaboration.

Indeed, words such as *management*, *colleague*, *collaborator*, and *support* are related to this cluster, as participants in their stories related the organizational transformation to their daily jobs. Figure 4.22 shows this analysis, indicating that it is not just a matter of the concepts used on average, but also how participants moved together across different clusters of words: from the words in the blue cluster to those in the orange clusters. This means that by transforming individually, they also transformed as a collective. Thus, the transformation process they embraced triggered the innovation process. They problematized their transformation to understand what it means to embrace the opportunity of digital transformation while remaining at the center (Figure 4.23).

4.5 Findings – how did transformation happen?

Organizational transformation requires all members to be engaged in collectively achieving the new objectives. Hence, we tracked the

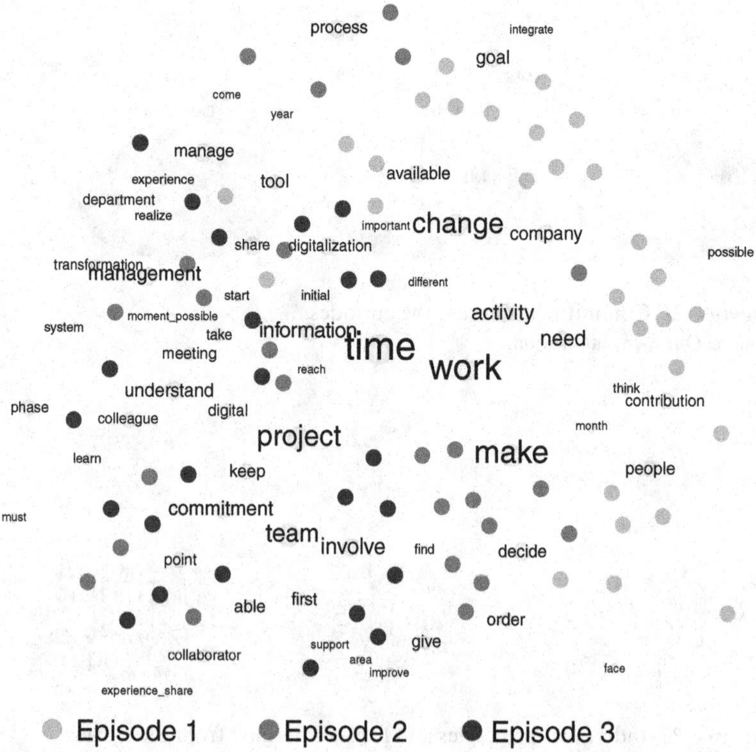

Figure 4.23 The evolution of the stories.
Source: Our own elaboration.

evolution of individual engagement in the transformation project (see Chapter 3 on measurement). The engagement path that emerged in these workshops is extremely interesting. Participants started the journey with a high level of engagement (4.3 out of 5). As they engaged in the storymaking experience and began to commit to making change happen, their level of engagement gradually grew throughout the entire process.

Further, we analyzed how participants perceived their own story and whether they found it both reasonable and relevant to pursue the outlined transformation path. Increasing engagement over time is supported by the perceived meaningfulness of the stories written by participants: we observed a high and stable perception of meaningfulness (average 4.3). This perception of meaningfulness nurtured their engagement in the transformation: each time participants faced a new

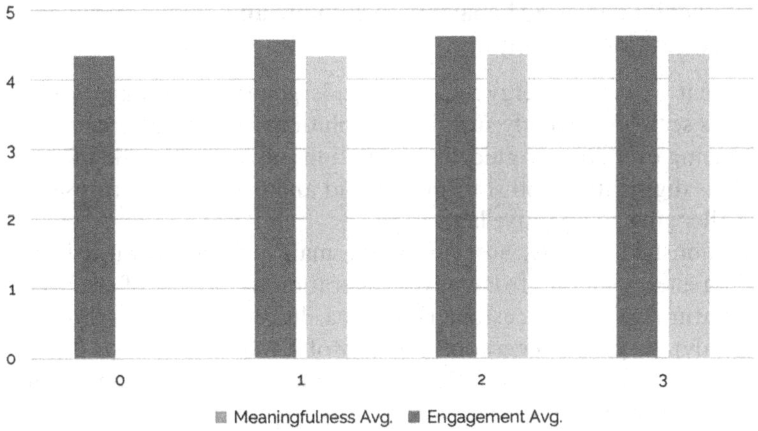

Figure 4.24 Engagement and meaningfulness.
Source: Our own elaboration.

obstacle, hurdle, or opportunity, and reflected on how to face it, they were able to make sense of it in their stories, and thus increase their overall understanding of the transformation and their engagement therein (Figure 4.24).

4.6 Conclusion and final reflections

The project implemented by the research team and Sintetica sparked commitment throughout the organization: 28 employees from all the main organizational functions and hierarchical levels took concrete action to understand how to embrace digital transformation in the human-centric organization. On average, the commitments participants made were fulfilled to a rate of over 3.2, further demonstrating high engagement in pursuing the transformation.

This project clearly shows that innovation calls for a gradual sense-making process. Participants made sense of what is needed to change along the journey. They moved from a broad and organizational perspective to a more relational and collaborative one where people are the only and real agents of transformation.

As they proceeded in this evolution by making sense of what was needed for their transformation, their engagement continuously increased. This clearly shows that before making things happen, they have to be meaningful to the individual, and if they are meaningful, they will spark action to make innovation happen.

5 Sorgenia: changing behaviors to embody an organizational meaning

In recent years, the energy sector has undergone radical changes. Customers seek increasingly sustainable solutions, and regulators are introducing ever-stricter guidelines. In addition, several market forces, such as digitization and shifting demand and prices, make this sector a challenging competitive landscape.

Established in 1999, Sorgenia is the main private operator in the Italian energy market from power generation to the sale of electricity and natural gas to end customers (with ca. 400,000 customers throughout Italy). Its power generation capacity of 4,400 MW consists of both natural gas plants with very low environmental emissions and plants from renewable sources.

Regarding the sale of electricity, gas, and services to end customers, Sorgenia has in recent years established and then consolidated its position as a top Italian digital energy company, a leader in innovation and the number of customers acquired through digital channels in the residential and business segments. The value proposition includes a clear offering, convenience, and simplicity, in addition to a focus on innovative services and core environmental values.

In the past five years, Sorgenia also developed a diversified portfolio of projects for renewable energy power plants: geothermal, hydroelectric, photovoltaic, wind, and biomethane. The commitment to the construction of renewable energy power plants is not only an industrial strategic decision, but also based on taking responsibility and a mission entirely focused on sustainability.

Over the past years, Sorgenia has worked hard to define a new organizational meaning, such as a novel purpose, a new interpretation of what is valuable to people. Following internal reflection, the company has made its mission to take care of the environment and have a positive impact on wider society. Two characteristics pave the way for a meaningful organizational transformation: innovation and inclusion. On the one hand, Sorgenia aims to pursue a path of discovery, pushing the boundaries to make energy accessible to everyone, on the other hand, living the dream of an inclusive organization as a group of diverse people who collaboratively search for novel paths.

5.1 The challenge

Sorgenia aimed to turn this aspirational meaning into a tangible organizational solution. As a group of diverse individuals working together, the leadership team realized that it was necessary to engage people in making the new meaning happen. A strategic shift had been suggested, but it was down to people to make the change come true. Sorgenia thus faced the challenge of designing a pathway to help every member of the organization understand the new direction and contribute to succeeding in the strategic shift.

The research platform delivered an idyllic environment for such a project. Through the storymaking experience, participants would design a story aimed at making the new meaning of the organization come true in their daily job. They would have the opportunity to suggest changes in their routines and discuss their plans with peers and supervisors, creating a motivated core team that would embody the new organizational meaning. Twenty-two participants were involved in this first phase: they were the kernel of change and conducted two months of research focusing on how to embody the organizational meaning in their daily actions.

5.2 *The storymaker workshop*

5.2.1 Setting the storyworld

Due to the high participation of members of the organization in the phase of envisioning the new meaning in previous projects, defining the reasons behind the change was an easy task. Indeed, the meaning had been defined in previous workshops as a set of three key characteristics: the set of *values* to pursue, the *principles* informing the new meaning, and the *meaning statement*. Through this visualization, the challenge was defined: the values are key pillars to maintain throughout the transformation, the *principles* help in defining areas of change for the transformation to come true, and the meaning is itself at the heart of the challenge.

The Brief: We live in a world full of change, opportunities, and challenges. The overcrowded market has raised competitive pressure, and the growth of the digital market is driving the need to find and communicate a clear direction to people.

Sorgenia decided to define a brief that would help individuals and the organization as a whole understand the implications of its meaning. Hence, the brief asked individuals to reflect on their work routines and habits that would need to change if the meaning was not to remain abstract but made tangible in their daily jobs. The organizational transformation would then follow as the workshop participants become catalysts of the new organization. The brief thus focused on individual change, asking participants to reflect on their behaviors to change with the question: *How do I have to change my behaviors to embody the meaning of Sorgenia in my daily job?*

The Pillars: The Sorgenia leadership and the research teams jointly identified three categories of values with two pillars each: the desire to *reshape the future*, the *role of the individual,* and the *organizational purpose.* These are deemed pivotal to the transformation journey and in crafting the participants' stories:

- *Our choices change the world.* The first pillar concerns the willingness to innovate: the organizational direction is embodied in the choices everyone makes.
- *Being an organization means building the future.* The organization pursues a vision, and each member can contribute to building the envisioned future together.
- *Responsibility is a life teacher.* Social and personal responsibility guide the choices people make and help identify the correct path for growth.
- *We transform complexity into easy solutions.* A complex environment should not mean that customers have to face difficulties: the organization takes these onto itself to deliver a simple solution.
- *The energy you put in is what matters.* The effort everyone is willing to put into innovating is what makes transformation happen: engagement matters, as does the concrete desire to make change come true.
- *Digital is the means, not the end.* Digitalization also has a key role: new digital technologies should be an enabling mechanism, a means to an end, and not the final objective (Figure 4.25).

What can be left behind: The Sorgenia leadership and the research teams jointly defined a set of areas of improvement, including the relationship with customers, knowledge management, and the innovation processes.

- *Being good not only at responding to customer requests, but anticipating them, being proactive.* First, in relating to customers, participants were challenged to go beyond merely responding to individual requests, developing anticipatory dynamics where each person works on suggesting novel solutions rather than sticking to mere problem-solving.
- *Do not put know-how before everything else: Look at the big picture. Understand why you are doing something and go to the heart*

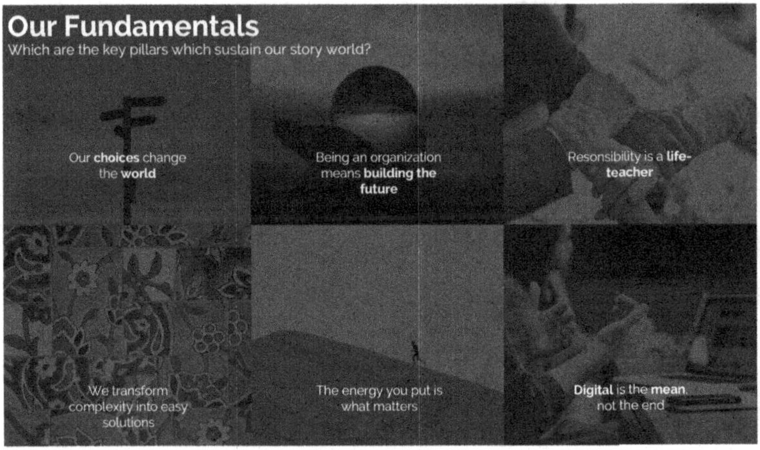

Figure 4.25 Sorgenia's storyworld: our fundamentals.
Source: Our own elaboration; images from Unsplash.com.

of it. Know-how should yield a more holistic view, inspiring a 360-degree overview of the change, thus leading to a deeper understanding of the rationale behind organizational choices.

- *Relying exclusively on experience: Support yourselves with data and take nothing for granted.* The team pointed to the role of data in challenging the status quo, reframing problems based not only on experience, but on the available information (Figure 4.26).

5.2.2 The storymaking journey

Also in Sorgenia, participants used the storymaker card set to write their individual transformation stories. Based on the aforementioned challenge, participants would design their prospective stories of transformation with the purpose of making sense of change and understanding how to make the novel meaning come true in their daily business.

5.3 Results – what happened?

5.3.1 How does change come true?

Participants set themselves a long-term objective, defining how they would have to change to respond to the organizational need. Throughout the four workshops, participants worked on making this transformation come true, reflecting on the organizational situation, and

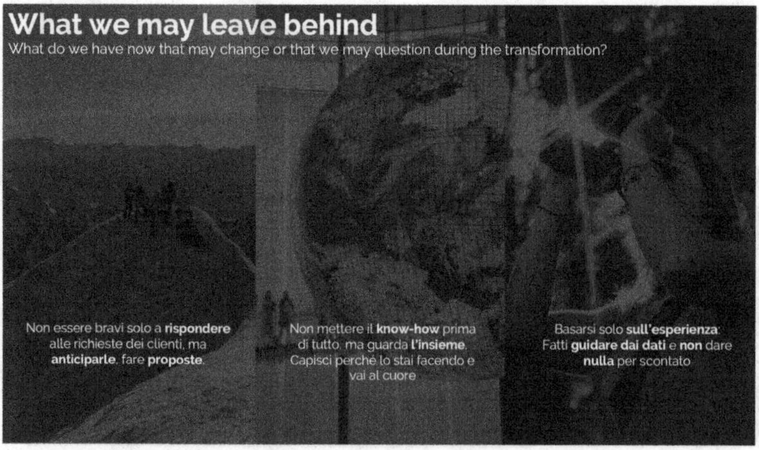

Figure 4.26 Sorgenia's storyworld: what we can leave behind.
Source: Our own elaboration; images from Unsplash.com.

making one small specific commitment to action that would provide the starting point for reflection in the subsequent workshop, as explained in Chapter 3. We found that the tendency of committing to small actions increased: in the first episode, over 40% of participants aimed to acquire new skills or influence other people. This percentage decreased to just around 10% after two months as the tendency to commit to concrete small actions increased. This confirms the aforementioned perception that the highest obstacle remained the self: participants made very small commitments, so they would be more manageable and easier to confront.

In addition to identifying their long-term objectives, participants were asked to reflect on the main obstacles they expected to face and some items or people who might prove helpful on their journey as *companions* sharing their burden, or as *mentors* providing guidance (see Chapter 3).

We found that over the months, participants identified several obstacles or personal hurdles: while in the first episode, almost 50% identified an external obstacle related to technologies or adequate partners for change, this percentage decreased to below 30% after two months. This underlines participants' increased sense of awareness and responsibility in the course of the transformation: changing first their way of being to addressing external challenges more effectively.

Interestingly, in Sorgenia the selection of companions and mentors was homogeneously distributed throughout the stories, with an adoption rate of around 66%. Worth noting is that the number of mentors selected remained stable throughout the process, whereas participants increased the number of companions they selected throughout the different episodes.

Almost one out of four stories (75%) considered the selection of a tool necessary for transformation, both digital (50%) and physical, thus underlining the value of external support to manage the tasks and plan activities.

5.4 What do your stories tell us?

The participants wrote their narratives to reflect on their individual transformation. To highlight the main values of these stories, they were asked to identify three principles reflecting the salient points. These principles sum up the driving forces behind the change, while the longer stories define *how* the transformation was achieved (see Chapter 3).

In the first episode, we could not identify common trends in how the principles were defined by either individuals or groups: many contrasting ideas and perspectives prevailed, without following a common thread. However, in the subsequent episodes, two main streams emerged: while the principles related to a positive attitude toward change, equilibrium, and passion remained in both episodes, some more polarized aspects manifested. Episode 2 witnessed the emergence of *collaboration* as people working together and *courage* as the desire to make bold choices. In episode 3, two principles emerged: *determination* to see the courageous choices through to the end, and *growth*, the natural consequence of a new-formed identity within a team.

The participants' stories followed a surprising path: while in the first episode, no common topic could be identified, the later stages brought forth two main topics. Figure 4.27 shows the word-clouds of the most used principles and words in the stories (see Chapter 5 for further explanations). On the one hand, *people* had a central role. One group of stories focused on the human side of the transformation process whereby the topics of *development*, *understanding*, and *learning* were central to stories throughout the episodes (in Figure 4.28, bottom cluster in orange). On the other hand, the second set of stories focused on making meaning actionable through actions and projects. From a more goal-oriented perspective, participants focused on finding

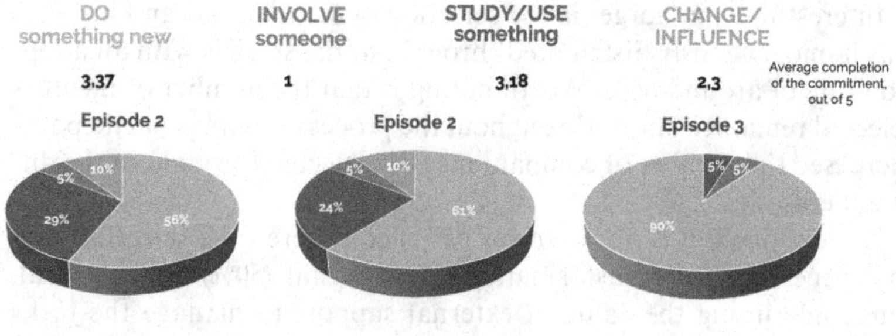

Figure 4.27 Commitments across the episodes.
Source: Our own elaboration.

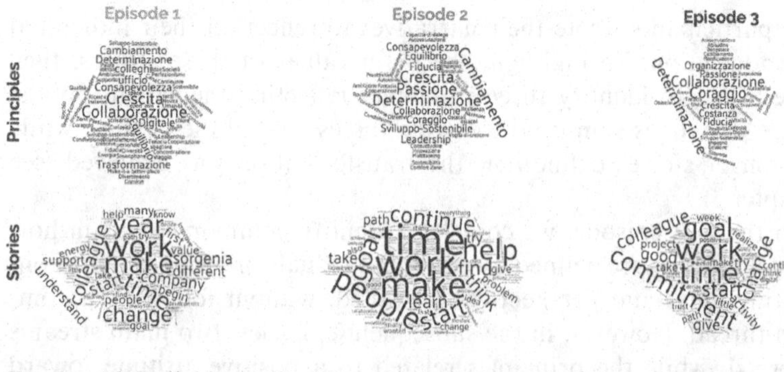

Figure 4.28 Individual principles and topics emerging from the stories.
Source: Our own elaboration.

concrete projects and paths to explore with colleagues to make the stories come true (Figure 4.28, top cluster in light blue). The concepts of *work* and *time* remained central in all stories: essential to any approach to change is dedication and continuous work on enacting the story.

Further, this confirms the previous findings on the principles: on the one hand, linked to the human side of change (*collaboration* and *growth*), and on the other hand, reinforcing the willingness to advance the projects (*courage* and *determination*) (Figure 4.29).

5.5 Findings – how did transformation happen?

Organizational transformation requires all members to collectively engage in achieving the novel objectives. Hence, we tracked the evolution of individual engagement in the transformation project (see Chapter 3

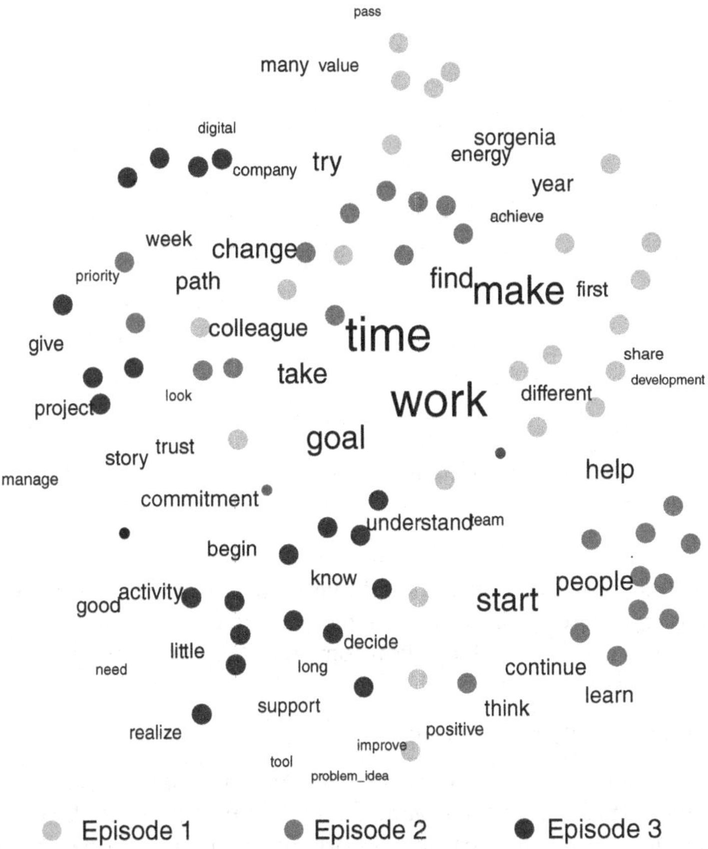

Figure 4.29 The evolution of the stories.
Source: Our own elaboration.

on measurement). As the new meaning had been defined in previous workshops, engagement in the project was very high from the very early phases with a value of 4, hence difficult to increase. Nonetheless, engagement further increased after the first episode in which the transformation stories were designed and shared for the first time. We then analyzed how participants perceived their own stories and whether they found it both reasonable and relevant to pursue the outlined transformation path. The perception of meaningfulness of the story remained constant throughout the first two episodes, while it increased suddenly after the last. In this final episode, participants' engagement again saw an increase. Hence, we assume that engagement in this company is also

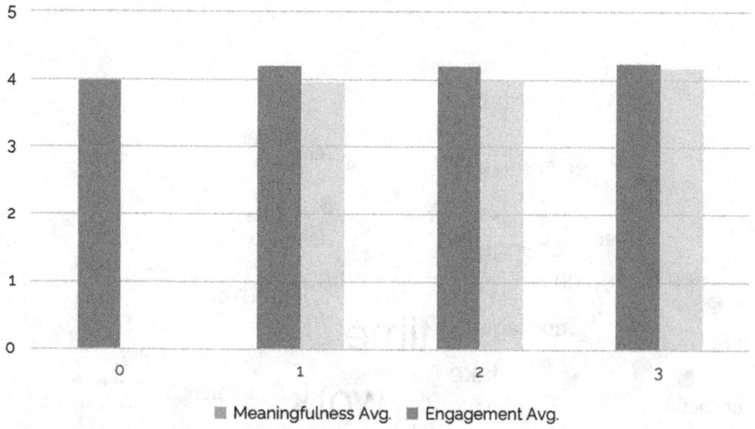

Figure 4.30 Engagement and meaningfulness.
Source: Our own elaboration.

linked to the perception of meaningfulness: the more they believe in their story and perceive it as rich in sense and purpose, the more they engage in making the transformation come true (Figure 4.30).

5.6 Conclusion and final reflections

The project implemented by the research team and Sorgenia sparked commitment throughout the organization: 22 participants took concrete action to make the meaning of Sorgenia come true. In particular, this project showed that there are multiple ways to take concrete action, starting from people, and outlining tangible transformation paths. On the one hand, participants recognized that for the organization to change, personal transformation was necessary. These stories hence focused on understanding, sharing, and learning, with great emphasis on supporting others and positive thinking. On the other hand, the stories also focused on outlining a tangible path for change: starting from the current Sorgenia context as an energy company, during the episodes, the stories increasingly focused on at least trying and finding concrete projects to work on together with colleagues.

Constant throughout all the stories, the topics of time and work underline the dedication needed for such a transformation. Setting goals is thus fundamental to change, both personal and as an organization, and sharing this path with a partner in an intimate relational environment is what makes the change meaningful and engaging.

6 STEF: designing new routines to foster the introduction of a new work model

In recent years, the food delivery market has undergone drastic changes. Market trends, such as digitization and greater interest in sustainability, have reshaped the competitive landscape, and logistics operators are required to be increasing reactive in responding to market demands.

In 1983, the STEF group took its first steps in Italy. Since then, its continuous growth has been fueled by numerous partnerships and acquisitions. Today, STEF holds a leading position in the controlled temperature logistics and transportation market, linking agri-food production with the world of consumers throughout Europe.

STEF is guided by experience, skill, and specialization: the orientation toward performance and customer service has guided the company's development over the last decades. In addition, recent years have seen the emergence of the socially responsible side of STEF: with close to 70% of employees owning part of its share capital, the company is responsible not only from a financial and environmental perspective, but also attributes a fundamental role to employee engagement.

STEF is today considered among the European specialists for temperature-controlled transportation and logistics of agri-food products. Although a multinational, its clear social commitment guides every decision.

6.1 The challenge

STEF recently conducted an internal analysis to identify and rationalize some strategic points of difference with respect to competitors. Among these, the company leadership identified a gap in time- to-market (TTM), i.e., responsiveness to new customers. The ability to respond to new market requirements in a timely manner was identified as a cross-functional requirement, hence an integrative approach to change. After a detailed analysis of the business processes, they identified a series of digital instruments that would enable a more flexible customer orientation, connecting different departments to reduce TTM.

In line with the values, this organizational transformation could not be implemented without first ensuring the engagement of people. As the first step, the leadership team organized an engagement workshop with those who would be directly involved in the first wave of change aimed at designing a new work model to be implemented in the following months based on an external digital tool. As the second step, the work model would be presented to individuals from different functional areas in the organization. The transformation process would therefore not be exclusively organizational, but also individual, and the research platform was selected as the ideal setting to perform this transformation journey. In this second phase, participants would envision their role in the organization after the introduction of the new work model.

6.2 The storymaker workshop

6.2.1 Setting the storyworld

Participants in the second phase had not been previously engaged in defining the new work model. Hence, the storyworld needed to clearly outline the purpose of the organizational and individual transformation to come.

The Brief: We live in a dynamic world in which the start of new services requires always lower TTM. STEF has the objective of eliminating process redundancies through a careful, unique, and transparent workflow re-design enabled by digital instruments to provide a holistic overview that allows everyone to contribute to the start-up of new services.

We desire a system of dashboards to engage people and enable them to deliver new solutions. Hence, you should ask yourselves: *How do you need to change, and what do you need to learn to do to exploit the potential of the new work model and increase TTM performance?*

The Pillars: The STEF leadership and the research team identified the organizational values synthesized in three keywords: *respect* for others' ideas, *enthusiasm* for growth, and a focus on *performance.* These were deemed pivotal to guiding the transformation journey, and hence in crafting the participant's stories:

- *Respect, the desire to listen to everyone's ideas and contributions.* The first value of the stories relates to respect for peers. All ideas should be accepted and critically discussed to allow everyone's contribution to the organizational transformation.
- *Enthusiasm, participation in the growth and success of projects and ideas that may not be mine or my team's.* The transformation should be characterized by enthusiasm for change. Everyone should be engaged in changing and motivated to achieve the successful implementation of ideas, regardless of their origin, be it their own or from another team member.

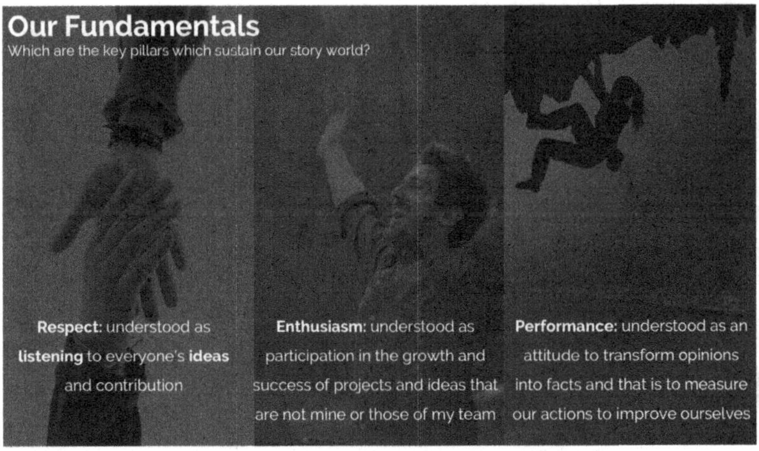
Our Fundamentals
Which are the key pillars which sustain our story world?
Respect: understood as listening to everyone's ideas and contribution
Enthusiasm: understood as participation in the growth and success of projects and ideas that are not mine or those of my team
Performance: understood as an attitude to transform opinions into facts and that is to measure our actions to improve ourselves

Figure 4.31 STEF's storyworld: our fundamentals.
Source: Our own elaboration; images from Unsplash.com.

- *Performance, the attitude to transform opinions into facts, and measuring our actions to better ourselves.* Last but not least, the focus of the stories should be a performance improvement, both tangible and measurable, so as not to remain abstract.

What can be left behind: The research team helped the leadership team define a selection of potential areas for improvement based on recent meetings that had identified three areas of transformation the company should focus on in the subsequent years.

- The leadership does not have all the answers: True leaders are not those who hold a dominant position, but those who listen to their collaborators. First, the role of the company leadership could undergo a change, as leaders do not have all the answers. Indeed, in a world in which openness to ideas and flexibility are reshaping the market environment, listening to co-workers and peers becomes a necessary leadership skill.
- Customers do not exclusively concern with the sales department, but the whole company, they are not the enemy, but a vector of potential personal, professional, and business development. Second, the role of customers should be radically revised to become the responsibility of the company as a whole, not one specific

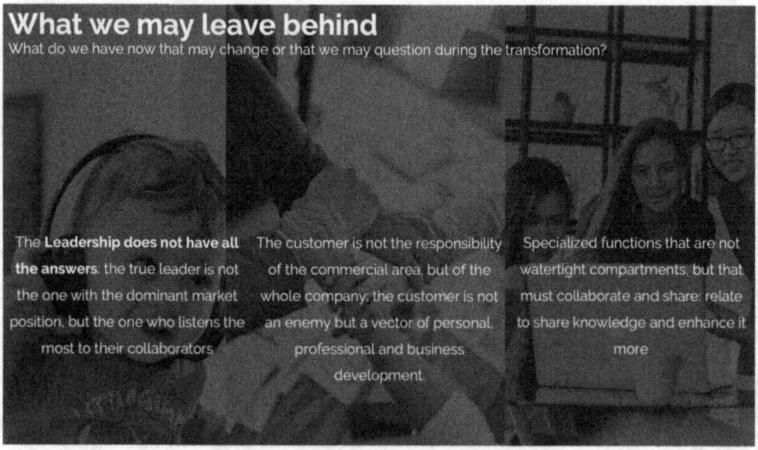

Figure 4.32 STEF's storyworld: what we can leave behind.
Source: Our own elaboration; images from Unsplash.com.

department, and seen as a source of personal, professional, and business growth for the whole organization.

- Specialized functions should not be hermetically sealed, but should collaborate, share knowledge, and value them more. Last, all departments should be engaged in the transformation horizontally, achieving collaboration and sharing instead of the more traditional silo structure (Figure 4.32).

6.2.2 The storymaking journey

In STEF, a simplified version of the storymaker card set was applied where all participants wrote their individual transformation stories, but without changing or updating them. Hence, the sensemaking process would be limited to a first in-depth reflection on the transformation to come.

6.3 Results – what happened?

6.3.1 How does change come true?

Participants set themselves a long-term objective, defining how they would need to change to respond to the transformation, reflecting on the organizational situation, and making one small specific commitment to action that would provide the starting point for reflection in the concluding episode (reduced version of the process depicted in Chapter 3). The commitments that participants selected were in line with these findings: only half the participants actually selected concrete actions to make change happen. The remainder desired to collaborate and share experiences and perspectives to increase their knowledge and understanding of the transformation process.

In addition to identifying their long-term objectives, participants were asked to reflect on the main obstacles they expected to face and some items or people who might prove helpful on their journey as *companions* sharing their burden, or as *mentors* providing guidance (see also Chapter 3).

Participants recognized that throughout the transformation process they would face obstacles related to both their personal characteristics and organizational inertia. This highlights that the implementation of a cross-functional team faces two types of resistance: on the one hand, the organization must be structurally prepared for the new way of working, on the other hand, individuals must determine how they need to change to accommodate the transformation.

The percentage of those selecting a companion for this transformation journey was striking: more than 80% of participants expressed the desire to select a companion, identifying either their team as a whole or a specific colleague. Only around 50% of participants desired a specific tool, and of these, one in four desired to acquire new skills. In total, 67% of participants selected a mentor to guide them in the transformation process.

6.4 *What do your stories tell us?*

The participants wrote their narratives to reflect on their individual transformations. To highlight the main value of these stories, they were asked to identify three principles reflecting the salient points. These principles sum up the driving forces behind the change, while the longer stories represent *how* the transformation was achieved (see Chapter 3).

The principles that participants selected for their stories in the first episode expressed one key concern: the desire to face the transformation challenge as a collaborative endeavor. Indeed, the principles selected were related mainly to inter-personal aspects such as *trust* and *listening*, while the emergent aspect of *change* was closely linked to the principle of *sharing*.

Figure 4.31 shows the word-clouds of the most frequently used principles and words in the stories (see Chapter 5 for further explanations).

In the single episode performed with STEF, three main conceptual areas emerged from the stories. In particular, the management identified three perspectives of participants to address the forthcoming transformation process: a personal dimension, the desire to take the initiative and implement a change project. First, participants recognized that organizational transformation requires first of all a change in individual perspectives. Hence, multiple stories discussed the need to see the long-term objectives of change while keeping the decisions shared. Second, some stories discussed the selection and development of novel ideas. Therefore, the new work model should provide an opportunity to leverage the perspectives and experiences of colleagues to develop new ideas that would not have been feasible in the previous organization. Last, some stories focused more on the development of the change project, the re-definition of the way of working, and the organizational habits to design a new organization in line with the new work model (Figure 4.33).

The participants' organizational transformation stories expressed the deep desire to make the most of the changing environment, change is seen as an opportunity to weave new ideas into the novel work model as long as it is linked to close collaborative relationships with colleagues.

6.5 *Findings – how did transformation happen?*

Measuring only the starting point of transformation in STEF did not allow tracking the progress as in the other partner organizations.

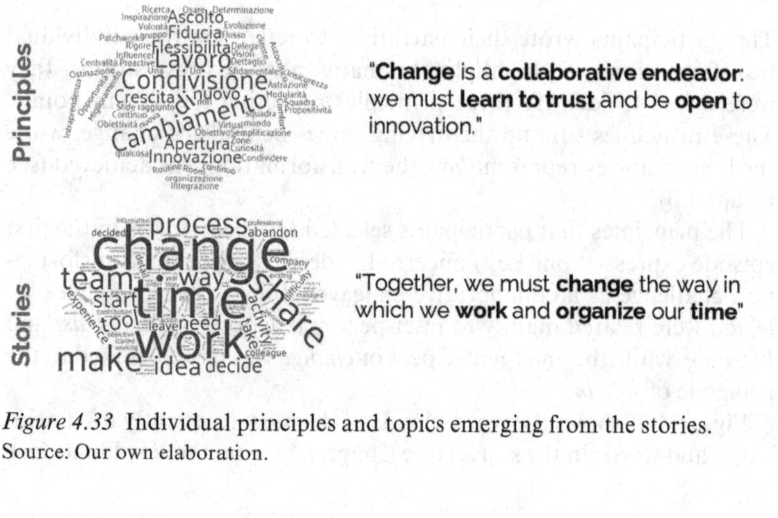

Figure 4.33 Individual principles and topics emerging from the stories.
Source: Our own elaboration.

Thus, a deeper analysis was conducted on participants in terms of *engagement* in the brief and *organizational citizenship*, i.e., support for the organization, comparing the values before and after the storywriting experience.

Almost half the participants could be described as *promoters* of the organization, as both their engagement in the project and citizenship behavior toward STEF increased throughout the experience. Writing the story of transformation contributed to a better understanding of the project and fostering a closer bond while also increasing appreciation for STEF. Interesting to note is that engagement in the transformation project was related to the perception of meaningfulness of their own story: only those individuals who perceived their story as averagely meaningful did not experience an increase in engagement in the project.

6.6 Conclusion and final reflections

In STEF, participants from different functional backgrounds were selected to design their transformation story. The purpose of the workshop was to spark commitment and involve diverse participants to understand and develop ideas related to the introduction of a new work model. While commitment could not be measured in subsequent interactions, we observed that merely writing their stories affected their engagement in the change project.

The stories focused on two main aspects: the opportunities provided by the new work model in terms of individual entrepreneurial behavior, and the desire for collaboration. Indeed, the partnering dimension was highly present throughout the different measurements: participants desired a companion for the transformation to share their aspirations and goals with a colleague or team.

5 Insights from the Research

1 Introduction

In this chapter, we explore the research platform structure in more detail. Whereas the previous chapter analyzed each project in detail, we now conduct a collective analysis.

We aim to present aggregate reflections illustrating how each project is linked to the overall platform. The chapter is organized as follows: first, we present the evolution of stories throughout the episodes, briefly describing the characteristics of each project. These are then integrated with an analysis of the fulfillment of commitments that participants made at the end of each episode.

Thereafter, we illustrate the evolution of the engagement and meaningfulness measures, comparing the specific cases, and drawing implications for the storymaking methodology and its relation to sensemaking theory.

As we mentioned in the opening, the project worked as a research platform that let us explore a few additional research areas critical to the understanding of transformation, namely, the interface between cognition and innovation, intimacy and innovation, convergence in the creation of a shared direction. In collaboration with our partner companies, we launched three additional research studies that are based on more of a Mode 1 research paradigm within our Mode 2 overarching research in progress. We delve into the details of the platform's three specific research streams to investigate the link among *cognition and innovation*, *the role of intimacy in innovation*, and the relevance of *converging in a shared direction*. For each, we discuss how the specific stream was implemented in terms of the research design and the preliminary results of the data analysis. Coghlan and colleagues (2020) argue that integrating Mode 1 research practice in Mode 2-based research projects is likely to enhance the scientific rigor, relevance, and

DOI: 10.4324/9781003276210–5

impact. Last, we highlight implications for managers pursuing organizational transformation, outlining four steps that facilitate the sense-making process in a context of innovation: (1) *setting the direction,* (2) *starting with small and relevant steps,* (3) *being critical,* and (4) *changing with someone else.*

2 The evolution of stories

The transformations accomplished by participants consisted of two main elements: the written stories that envisioned their future transformation, and the concrete commitments made at the end of each episode.

First, we briefly introduce the content of the stories that participants wrote throughout the experiences. As explained in more detail in the *Cognition and innovation* section, our analysis focused on the most common words in each story and the latent topics extracted in a machine-learning approach. Table 5.1 summarizes the content of the three episodes for each company through word-clouds and a short comment providing further details on how the stories evolved.

All five companies shared similar paths. Throughout the episodes, the concepts of dedicating *time* and *work* to the transformation were relevant for all participants. These increased in mention in the last episodes, whereas initially the stories were dominated by organizational-level concepts describing the organizational need to change. Hence, the initial workshops helped participants reframe the goal of their personal transformation project, while in the subsequent episodes, the transformation projects became real. As the experience guided them in their reflection, participants naturally tended to become increasingly practical and active in the transformation process.

The commitments provided a complementary view to the content of the stories. While participants envisioned their transformation through written stories, they enacted it through a set of small actions. At the end of each episode, participants picked a commitment, a concrete action to be fulfilled in the following two to three weeks that would serve as the starting point for the subsequent episode. Table 5.2 summarizes the average fulfillment rate for each company and each episode on a scale of 1 to 5. On average, participants succeeded in completing their commitment. The reasons for incompletion and the challenges faced were the inputs of the reasoning for the subsequent episodes.

Overall, the fulfillment rate increased throughout the episodes: as participants revised their commitments, they chose increasingly specific actions. While the initial commitments were very ambitious and

Table 5.1 Evolution of the stories and principles for each organization

<table>
<tr><th>Partner</th><th colspan="3">Evolution of stories throughout the episodes</th></tr>
<tr><th></th><th>Episode 1</th><th>Episode 2</th><th>Episode 3</th></tr>
<tr><td>Nestlé</td><td>
</td><td>
</td><td>
</td></tr>
<tr><td></td><td colspan="3">The concept of people was particularly relevant throughout the stories. This is coherent with the challenge of understanding how each participant could grow to be an innovative leader. The initial stories were very abstract, talking about the innovation concept, the role of people, and their willingness to change. Interestingly, in the last episode, the focus shifted toward the team to collaborate on shared projects.</td></tr>
<tr><td>Philips</td><td>
</td><td>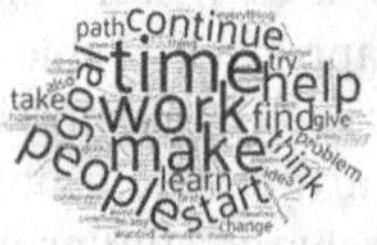
</td><td>
</td></tr>
<tr><td></td><td colspan="3">The topics of finding new solutions and making things happen were transversal throughout the episodes with different nuances. In the second episode, the need to collaborate as a team emerged where everyone committed to working hard to make change happen. Finally, in the third episode, the need for a dedicated and scheduled time became central alongside team collaboration to jointly immerse and reflect on how to change.</td></tr>
<tr><td>Sasol</td><td>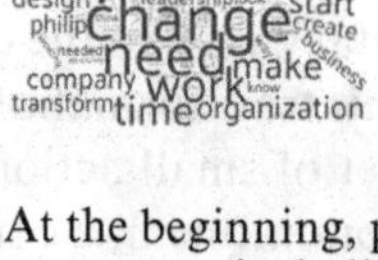
</td><td>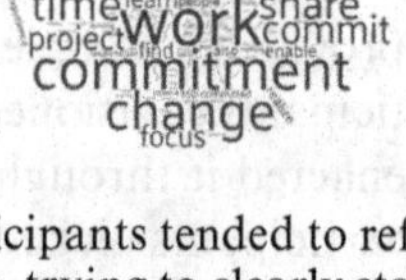
</td><td>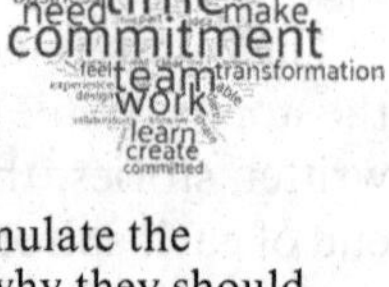
</td></tr>
<tr><td></td><td colspan="3">At the beginning, participants tended to reformulate the company's challenge, trying to clearly state why they should use 10% of their time to innovate. The stories remained on an abstract level. In the second episode, the time and commitment dimensions tended to emerge. Interestingly, the words in the third episode were highly oriented toward execution: how they are changing their behaviors and how they can make the transformation happen.</td></tr>
</table>

Table 5.1 Continued

<table>
<tr><th>Partner</th><th colspan="3">Evolution of stories throughout the episodes</th></tr>
<tr><th></th><th>Episode 1</th><th>Episode 2</th><th>Episode 3</th></tr>
<tr><td>Sintetica</td><td>
</td><td>
</td><td>
</td></tr>
<tr><td></td><td colspan="3">Work and time were two central concepts throughout the episodes. From an initial organizational dimension, understanding how the company needs to change, the stories become gradually more personal: first, describing the involvement of people in specific activities and projects, then focusing on the role of the team for specific change projects.</td></tr>
<tr><td>Sorgenia</td><td>
</td><td>
</td><td>
</td></tr>
<tr><td></td><td colspan="3">The topics of work and making change happen were present throughout the stories with different associations. First, it was about understanding the change, then starting to act, relations with people, and goals became more important. Last, to really start the change, commitment is central to making the goal happen.</td></tr>
</table>

Source: All images produced from our data using wordcloud.com.

Table 5.2 Fulfillment of commitments

	Episode 1	*Episode 2*	*Episode 3*
Nestlé	3.11	3.21	3.31
Philips	3.06	3.18	3.30
Sasol	2.62	3.08	3.05
Sintetica	3.17	3.12	3.25
Sorgenia	3.19	3.25	3.31

related to acquiring new skills, in the later episode, the transformation was increasingly linked to other people. As people become more engaged in the transformation, they also become more dedicated to making change happen by contacting somebody they wish to change with.

Interestingly, Table 5.2 shows that while the average trend depicts an increasing fulfillment rate of commitments, some peculiar situations emerge. First, Sasol shows a slight decrease in the fulfillment rate from the second to the third episode. However, in the first episode, Sasol showed the lowest fulfillment rate, and therefore a steep increase following the low rate in the first period was difficult to exceed.

On the other hand, Sintetica shows a different pattern with a decrease in the fulfillment rate in the second episode to an increase in the final episode. The particular situation of this project, spread over multiple months and the holiday season, may reflect the intermediate low.

Despite these minor inconsistencies, the trend is a steady increase throughout the three storymaking episodes. In the following sections, we analyze the evolution of the *engagement* and *meaningfulness* indicators. These complement the story-related analyses, as we examine the participants' perceptions.

3 The evolution of engagement and meaningfulness

The main goal of the storymaking experience is engaging people in a transformation process to make innovation happen, considering engagement as an antecedent of concrete actions toward innovation.

Overall, we highlight two common trends. First, working on their own prospective transformation story led to a high level of meaningfulness from the very beginning. The meaningfulness indicator further increased over time in all cases. Engagement differed throughout the companies, but in all cases, the projects ended with a high engagement level. In Chapter 4, the evolution of the two variables over time is provided for each organization.

The challenge faced in the research presented in this book aimed not only at creating engagement, but also at keeping individuals engaged over time. This would allow a more unbiased measurement, as the effect of performing an unusual task (i.e., the workshop) would lose impact. In addition, the engagement measure would capture both the development of the transformation story and the effects of real-life events occurring between the episodes.

Hence, the storymaking experience embodies a two-fold success. First, creating engagement from the very beginning: the first measurement was performed after only the kick-off where participants described themselves and designed a direction. The new approach based on stories instead of images shows a positive effect on participant engagement.

Second, storymaking contributes to keeping people engaged over time. Indeed, in all projects, engagement measured at the end of the third episode was on average equal to the initial measurement. As transformation requires time to succeed, keeping people engaged is key to succeeding in changing an organization.

The success of the storymaking experience may in part relate to how individuals think of their stories. The measure of meaningfulness describes how individuals make sense of their environment by writing a story they relate to, thus envisioning their transformation. The case of Sasol is again emblematic in this sense: while engagement fell after the first episode, it increased again as individuals started perceiving their stories as more meaningful.

The research thus designs a path that not only creates momentary engagement but helps people progressively make sense of transformation. In the next sections, we will discuss the implications of these findings from both a theoretical and practical point of view.

4 Theoretical contributions

The analysis of the stories and the resulting changes in individual engagement allowed us to draw implications for theory. Indeed, our research aimed at creating value for both theory and practice. This is likely enhanced by integrating Mode 1 research orientations as was needed within a Mode 2 research project. Hence, we will first introduce the implications of this research for the innovation and sensemaking literature. Thereafter, we explore in more detail the distinct research streams characterizing the research platform.

We observed that the stories shifted from an abstract level to a more operational level in which individuals illustrated the necessary actions to make change happen. This first point offers relevant insights for the innovation literature. Extant research investigates the role of stories as a communication tool (Denning, 2006; Bartel & Garud, 2009) and facilitator of sensemaking (Cunliffe & Coupland, 2012). The shift from storytelling to storymaking led to a pragmatic effect. Indeed, transformation is achieved through gradual actions and changes in behavior, in addition to making sense of the new desired scenario (Denning, 2006; Hill et al., 2014). The creation of new narratives enables people to transform, update their cognitive frames, and coherently guide action (Weick, 1995; Blomquist & Lundin, 2010). In particular, the accomplishment of the commitments throughout the episodes helped participants gain familiarity with the innovation environment (Enninga & van der Lugt, 2016). The different actions nurtured the repeated reframing endeavor (Weick, 1995), sustaining the process of shaping new individual identities.

In this process, criticism plays a central role: participants were first asked to commit to specific actions and then to be critical of the achievement of their commitment. The literature acknowledges that the adoption of new norms and behaviors might cause discomfort in individuals undergoing change in the organizational context (Kleiner & Roth, 1997). For this reason, critical reflection of the commitment plays a fundamental role in enabling individuals to frame uncertainty and assimilate new external cues to enrich the sensemaking process (Stigliani & Ravasi, 2012). Throughout the sense perception process in which new meaning is continuously shaped and actualized, people are able to build confidence in facing hurdles and inertia (Humphreys & Brown, 2002).

Finally, the process of making sense of change through stories emerged as a compelling way to nurture engagement over time (Garcia Martinez, 2015). Throughout the experiences, stories became more meaningful as people perceived a deeper sense of clarity in framing and enacting the story. Maitlis and Sonenshein (2010) discuss the link between different types of change and how individuals make sense of it. Reluctance is often determined by emotional ties to the previous organizational identity, making change difficult, as managers must first overcome anchorage to the status quo before untangling the possibilities embedded in the innovation process. Innovating requires a strict commitment to move forward, which must come from individuals' internal drive: innovation requires an individual transformation process, pursuing a direction that is shared with other members of the organization. Designing new narratives helps them relate to the changing context and may facilitate individual transformation. In the storymaking experience, we identified several principles of sensemaking theory as a means of managing novel and uncertain scenarios (Table 5.3).

While the literature acknowledges that the approach to identifying an engaging story for people to make innovation happen is still under discussion (Denning, 2006), our study calls for further attention to the transformational nature of the meaning-making process where individuals are the primary actors of the transformation. Indeed, shifting from a perspective where stories are employed as a tool to transmit extrinsic business objectives (Denning, 2006; Green & Sergeeva, 2019), narratives can act as transformative means guiding individuals in shaping their desired identities within the organization (Humphreys & Brown, 2002; Cunliffe & Coupland, 2012). Next, we draw some conclusions for each vertical research streams identified in the previous sections.

5 Reflecting on the additional three research streams

The storymaking experience enabled incorporating three additional research streams benefitting from the structure that the storymaking

Table 5.3 Storymaking experience design principles

	Sensemaking under uncertainty	*Story-design principles*
Purpose	Building shared meanings in turbulent times	Creating a new organizational identity through individual transformation
Commitment	Commitment to a plan keeps people moving forward	Measuring engagement in a meaningful prospective narrative
Identity	Identity transformation throughout the process	Reflecting on individual characteristics
Direction	Expectations combine with cues to build new meaning	Envisioning a direction to pursue and turn into reality
Action	Action consolidates environmental elements	Making a series of small and manageable commitments
Cyclicity	Adaptive sensemaking to build shared meanings (*updating* and *doubting*)	Continuous reframing of commitments based on recent experiences

Source: Based on Weick (1995), Corley and Gioia (2004), Maitlis and Sonenshein (2010).

experience provides to explore additional dynamics. Specifically, the three research streams focus on: (i) cognition in innovation, intended as the sensemaking process through which groups of individuals construct a shared perspective of change; (ii) the role of intimacy in innovation, a stream aimed at investigating how collaborating in the intimacy of a pair fosters the individuals' understanding of change and their engagement therein; and (iii) convergence in innovation.

In what follows, we present the key findings from each specific research stream and the related implications.

5.1 Cognition and innovation

To make sense of change, individuals apply their existing cognitive frames to reading the environment (Weick, 1995; Maitlis & Christianson, 2014). Organizational transformation is the result of this framing process that takes place at the individual level initially and grows to form an organizational orientation. The way in which the environment changes though is not static: individuals change, and so does their understanding of a situation (Rhodes & Brown, 2005; Stigliani & Ravasi, 2012). Creativity and innovation are not only a managerial process, as they require transformation. The psychology literature has extensively contributed to understanding these processes (Csikszentmihalyi & Getzels, 1973; Perry-Smith & Mannucci, 2017; Aggarwal & Woolley, 2019).

This first vertical research stream aims to investigate how individuals make sense of change, and how this "sense" changes over time. This change is investigated through the analysis of written content, allowing us to study the evolution at both the individual and group level throughout the episodes.

We observed the sensemaking process from a quantitative perspective, analyzing the words emerging in the stories. As Maitlis and Sonenshein (2010) argue, language is a fundamental building block of the meaning individuals perceive: it is through language that we communicate our understanding to the extent that language and meaning are tightly coupled (Maitlis & Christianson, 2014). Indeed, sensemaking is a process of social construction in which a group creates new meaning through the use of a new language (Sandberg & Tsoukas, 2015). We analyzed the stories from two separate points of view: on the one hand, we analyzed the most common words using a word-cloud representation. In a word-cloud, the size of each word is proportional to the frequency with which participants mention that specific word. The analysis highlights the most common terms that participants used to describe their transformation journey. On the other hand, we performed a text-mining analysis, which allowed us to capture the longitudinal evolution of stories for each of the partner organizations. The text mining analysis was structured as follows:

1 *Data extraction.* Our analysis is based on two subsets of words extracted from the stories. First, we extracted the "salient" words (the ten words with the highest occurrence for each story), second, we adopted *latent Dirichlet allocation* (Blei et al., 2003) to extract a latent topic from each story, which led to ten additional keywords. We then further analyzed these 20 keywords.
2 *Data analysis.* We adopt a measurement system based on machine learning to extract sense from the stories. Word embeddings or word vectors represent words as vectors in an *n-dimensional space* and allow performing mathematical operations (Turian et al., 2010; Mikolov et al., 2013). This then enables combining multiple word vectors into a single one, representing each story as a single point in vector space (De Boom et al., 2016), and analyzing the centrality of the concepts and how stories unfold over multiple episodes. The principle of word vectors allows to perform mathematical operations on language. Imagine that you wish to

find the capital of Germany and wanted to describe this in terms of a mathematical equation starting from the Italian capital. The result would look something like this: "Rome" – "Italy" + "Germany" =? Word vectors analyze the language structure, and such a question would successfully provide the correct answer (Berlin). Now, while the usage of objective words such as city or country names is well known, inside smaller groups of individuals a new, shared language may emerge – with words taking on a slightly new meaning.

3 Our analysis tries to highlight this new meaning, providing a representation of how close (in terms of meaning) some words are to each other. If, for example, the word "innovation" lies close to the word "risk", this would express that individuals part of the group tend to see the dangers of changing their working habits; if, on the other hand, the word "innovation" was closer to "opportunity" or "growth", this would express a different frame – that of innovation as an open possibility. Figure 5.1 shows one of these analyses, in which the story of each individual is represented as a single circle. The position of this circle is linked to its meaning – that is, it is closer to the words which best summarize the story.

4 In our analysis, we recognized three common elements in all the stories. First, some concepts remained at the center of most stories in all companies throughout the three episodes, namely, *change, time,* and *work*. These three characteristics are at the core of any transformation process: achieving personal and organizational change requires dedicating much work and time to the activities that help this transition. Second, our results suggest the importance of human support. Interesting to note is that this support evolves greatly from the first to the last episode, becoming ever more intimate. While in the first episode, *people* are mentioned in general terms, in the second and third episodes, the stories revolve around the concepts of *colleagues* and *team*. This shows not only that transformation requires external support, but the more concrete the stories become, the more this support is sought in the closest individuals. The vector representation allows grasping not only the discrete perceptions about change, but also the dynamic dimension. Figure 5.1 shows the main words emerging from the stories where each point represents one story, with the color indicating the episode. Indeed, the stories progressively moved to the lower left of the figure: individual stories *collectively* moved from an initially very abstract and organizational dimension to a more concrete perspective on projects and meetings. The movement across the map

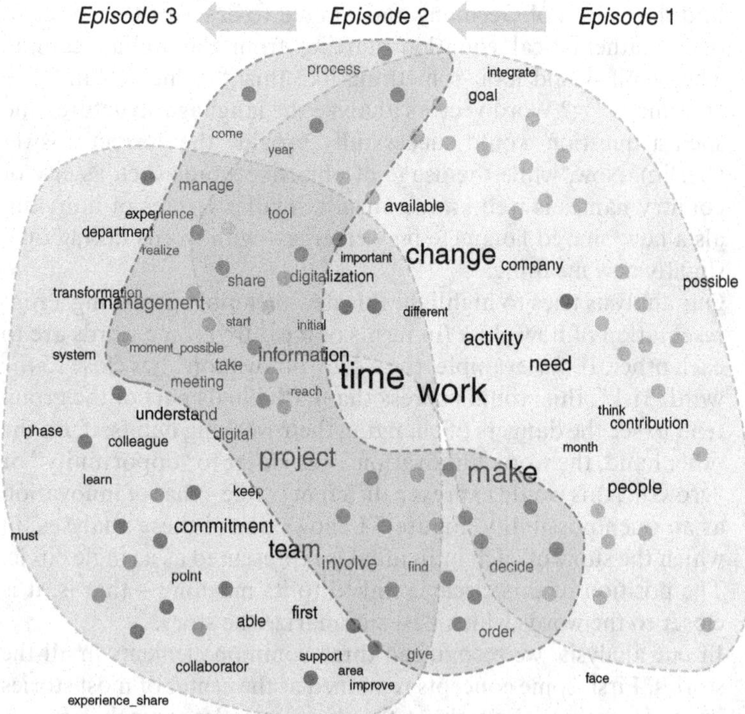

Figure 5.1 Word embeddings applied to the stories of Sintetica.
Source: Our own elaboration.

exemplifies that the sensemaking process constitutes not only an individual but a collective understanding of the transformation.

5.2 The role of intimacy in innovation

Among various group-based collaboration practices, pairs are emerging as a powerful way to foster innovation (Hunter et al., 2012; Rouse, 2020; Bellis & Verganti 2021). Pairs provide an intimate and safe psychological space of reflection where individuals feel free to share half-baked ideas, receive critical feedback, and therefore reframe (Farrel, 2003; Verganti, 2017). In addition, the sensemaking endeavor that innovation activities require benefits from a certain level of intimacy to establish comfortable communication that enables individuals to unveil new depth areas and create new connections among the ideas (Weick, 1995; Dougherty et al., 2000).

Therefore, this vertical stream aims to investigate how intimate moments of reflection in pairs support individuals' sensemaking (hence, their perception of meaningfulness) of their personal transformation journey. More precisely, in the previous sections, we explained how meaningfulness sustains engagement along the transformation journey. Here, the aim is to investigate how this perception of meaningfulness leads to leveraging moments of intimate reflection in pairs.

To explore these assumptions, in all the episodes, participants were given the opportunity to have a moment of collaborative reflection with a partner: working as a pair, participants had to mutually share the status of their stories, their main learnings, and hurdles from the experience, and how they intended to manage them. Each acted as a sparring partner, providing support in improving the other story by suggesting new ideas, integrating something that was missing, or highlighting some possible obstacles that might arise.

After each pair session, the individuals' perception of the intimacy experienced was assessed with scales used in the literature. In particular, we assessed two types of intimacy. First, the perception of relational intimacy (Roloff et al., 1988): a broader assessment of intimacy that enables understanding to what extent the two individuals are close friends or casual acquaintances. Second, we selected and adapted items from the interaction record form for intimacy (Prager & Buhrmester, 1998) to assess the specific situational intimacy that participants experienced during their interaction. Participants were asked to rate on a Likert-type scale (from 1 to 5) how well each statement described the interaction experienced with their partner.

The findings suggest that three main intimacy dimensions describe the interaction experienced within the pair: emotional intimacy (mutual self-disclosure of feelings and emotions), cognitive intimacy (mutual criticism, sharing of ideas, and reframing), and thoughtful intimacy (mutual attentive listening). These three elements appear critical to nurturing the individual perception of meaningfulness and subsequent engagement in moving toward the innovation journey (Figure 5.2).

In a sense, creating something meaningful is not a linear process, it is something that requires individual time, reflection, and immersion (Leonard & Sensiper, 1998). In addition, this vertical research stream shows that sensemaking benefits from intimate moments of collaboration where the individual feels protected and cared for by a trusted peer, where emotions and feelings can flow sustained by the demonstration of mutual caring and listening. Finally, intimate moments of collaboration enable mutual criticism, meaning the possibility to see

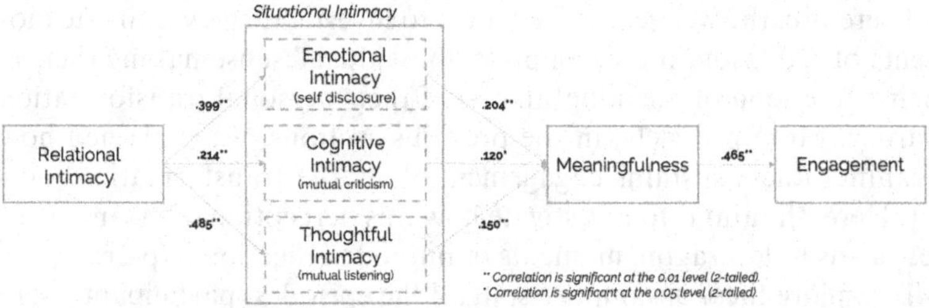

Figure 5.2 Results of the intimacy, meaningfulness, and engagement correlation.
Source: Our own elaboration.

the "world" situation through different lenses, learning, and therefore reframing.

Relational intimacy is an antecedent of these dynamics, an enabler of establishing good moments of interaction and exchange: a high level of relational intimacy indicates good sensitivity to other needs as well as the willingness to act toward them (Roloff et al., 1988).

5.3 *The role of convergence toward a new strategic direction*

To make innovation happen, people need to converge toward a new meaningful direction (Holloway, 2009; Verganti, 2017). As the articulation of transformation is a social process that requires the inclusion of multiple voices at different levels of the organization (Sanders & Stappers, 2008; Frow et al., 2015), individuals affected by the change need to remain engaged in the process (Shamiyeh, 2016).

While the literature acknowledges that collaboration plays a crucial role in maintaining a sense of cohesion among individuals (Paulus & Nijstad, 2003; Harvey, 2014), there is still a lack of studies on how the micro-dynamics influence convergence when individuals develop a collective interpretation (Fulmer & Ostroff, 2016).

This vertical research stream aims to investigate how selection and synthesis influence convergence when people in the organization articulate a new strategic direction. To provide a consistent answer, we conducted a longitudinal field experiment (Harrison & List, 2004) in six organizations taking part in the storymaking journey. Each collaborative method was randomly assigned a dyad of companies to compare the alternative ways through which individuals create shared knowledge, whether through filtering (Putman & Paulus, 2009) or integrating (Kolko, 2010; Harvey, 2014) different information over time.

To design the dynamics that enable people to converge toward a shared direction, we were inspired by the micro-dynamics regulating the flocking behavior of birds (Reynolds, 1987). Research has shown that appropriate behavioral rules for individuals can determine specific features of aggregation at the collective level. Each bird appears to compare its position and speed to those closest to it (6 or 7), making the required adjustments to maintain the flock's coherence (Ballerini et al., 2008). Hence, participants formed small sub-groups and reshuffled so as to contaminate each other as much as possible. The aggregation needs to be established within each sub-group, but at the same time propagated across the overall group of participants.

First, during each episode, we asked participants to synthesize their individual narratives into three keywords. At the end of each episode, we asked subgroups of participants to collectively define a set of shared principles underlying their stories, leveraging selection, or synthesis to converge at the group level. During the experiment, we collected data in the form of actual content created by participants (e.g., individual and group keywords): we analyzed the words in terms of frequency and occurrence in the episodes, while assessing people's tendency to select over time individual or group principles to describe their stories.

Based on our analysis, the results show that convergence is differently affected by multiple methods. In companies where selection was employed, a small set of keywords gained resonance over time, reaching a higher frequency of use. Here, open and abstract keywords were used by participants to include different perspectives as a final outcome. As a result, a form of static convergence emerged over time where individuals were able to construct a shared interpretation of the transformation by relying on a limited set of general and abstract concepts over time.

Instead, synthesis triggered the opposite effect on the creation of a common understanding of the change. Here, the evolving nature of the dialogue (Weick et al., 2005) led individuals to generate new specific and enriched keywords to integrate different perspectives in the process. As a result, a volatile and dynamic form of convergence emerged over time, as new concepts were continuously constructed to adapt the shared understanding to the new individuals joining the conversation over the episodes.

Interestingly, the use of the two alternative methods also had effects on the way people were likely to bring keywords from one episode to another. In other words, participants' willingness to propagate knowledge over time was influenced by the use of different ways of collectively making sense of information. In fact, while selection seems to

Table 5.4 Influence of selection and synthesis on emergence and convergence

Collaborative method	*Level of emergence*	*Convergence*	*Propagation of knowledge*
Selection	Macro-level (Weak form: abstract and open keywords)	General and stable	Tendency to propagate information generated individually
Synthesis	Micro-level (Strong form: specific and enriched keywords)	Local and dynamic	Tendency to propagate information generated collectively

foster people's tendency to over time select keywords generated individually, synthesis seems to trigger their willingness to iteratively select collectively generated concepts (Table 5.4).

In a world overcrowded with ideas, one of the biggest challenges is not finding an abundance of alternatives, but overcoming inertia due to too many ideas. This research provides insights for managers on how to orchestrate over time the complex ecology of micro-interactions among individuals to create a shared interpretation of a new direction of change.

6 Results for management

In line with the principles of action research and design science research, this research project offers relevant managerial implications. First, it helped the companies engage their employees in a transformation project. Specifically, in each partner organization, around 20–30 participants were engaged to think about and take concrete action toward the realization of an organizational transformation process. Throughout the three months, each organization benefited from around 50 individual actions, ranging from a personal growth experience to the joint development of new routines. Hence, through transforming themselves, the individuals gradually advanced the organizational transformation.

Second, four basic elements of the storymaking experience that engaged people and helped them go through their transformation emerged from the process. Together with the partner organizations, the research team developed a storymaking experience that may be applied in a similar or synthetic form to address individual transformation for organizational change. Therefore, this research contributed not only to the partner organizations and the workshop participants' identity creation but provided a broader spectrum of practitioners with the tools to facilitate employee transformation.

7 Takeaways for participants

As our final result, we identify the main implications for participants taking part in the experience. First, each started a transformation journey. While we acknowledge that the process is not over yet, the greatest challenge for transformation is the start. Having a set of small actions and commitments designed and shared with colleagues is a great starting point for both individual and organizational transformation.

Second, all participants have been exposed to a process, the storymaker workshop, which likely inspired their professional life. All partners have access to the toolkit to repeat this process anytime they need it.

This leads to our final great challenge for thought and reasoning: What is the real value participants derive from the project? Is it "just" what they have done and the chance to repeat it?

We believe the experience provided something more that embeds many relevant elements to make innovation happen, as shown through the storymaker experience. These concepts may outlast the experience itself and stay with participants longer, with or without the repetition of the specific experience.

Therefore, we have identified and outlined these elements as the basic ingredients to make transformation happen according to the principles that inspire the design of the process, as well as the insights we gathered in this year of research. Figure 5.3 summarizes the four elements.

1 *Setting your direction.* To start a meaningful transformation journey, people need to have a clear direction to follow. It may come from the organization, as in our case, or from a long-term goal each of us has. What matters most is that it needs to be reinterpreted to make it *your* direction of change.
2 *Starting with small, relevant steps.* Change is difficult, and reaching the final destination of the transformation journey overnight is impossible. To embrace a transformation journey, people should identify small but relevant steps to make the first jump into the unknown and start down the path. Identifying small concrete actions is essential to begin making them real.

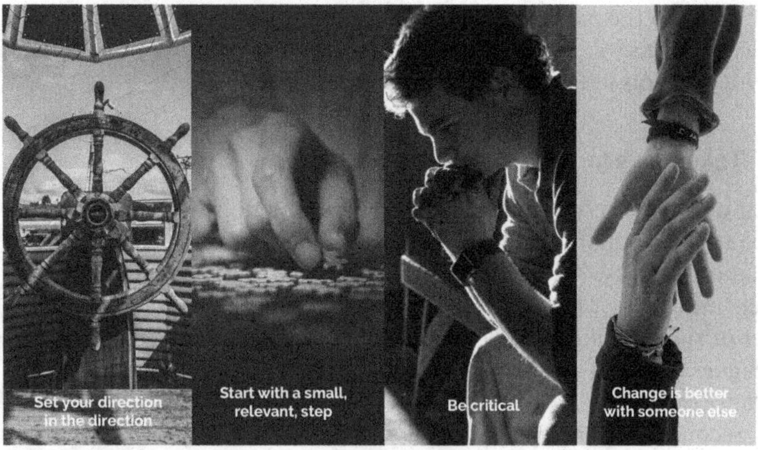

Figure 5.3 The four basic elements to make transformation happen.
Source: Images obtained from unsplash.com with a creative commons license.

3 *Being critical.* Criticism is the heart of innovation. Am I going in the right direction? Was it the right first step? Change is a continuous challenge, and each of us in her/his transformation journey may make a wrong decision. Being critical of any decision we make is essential to adapt and revise our journey and – why not? – even our own direction. Still, criticism needs to stay with us throughout the journey to help us make sense of our path.

4 *Changing with someone else.* Choosing a companion, mentor, peer to work in a pair, or colleagues to create a circle, no matter who, how, or when, because other people are fundamental in a transformation journey. We should not be scared of asking for help, opinions, and criticism from others who can contribute to making our journey more meaningful.

These are the four storymaking basic elements that we left all the participants with to hopefully guide their future transformation projects and enhance the diffusion of the implications of this research. Taking a step back, it is clear that these four elements constitute the pillars that informed the research project from the very beginning: innovation as meaning, design as engagement, and leadership as the community (Figure 5.4). In other words, innovation and design as leadership to embrace and make transformation happen.

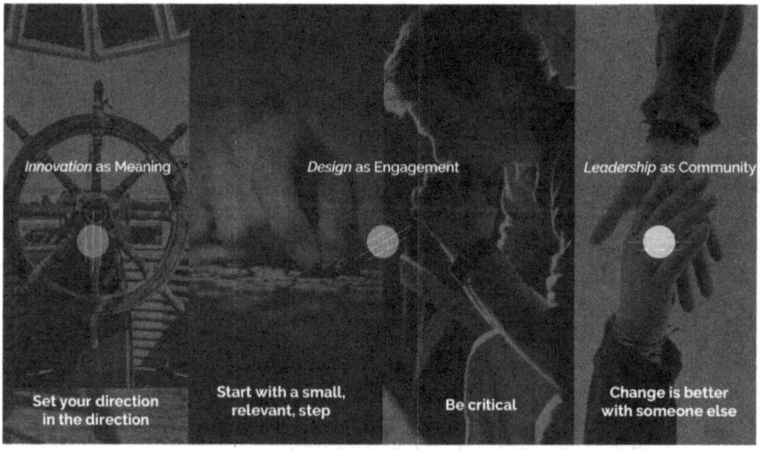

Figure 5.4 The four basic elements and the platform's principles.
Source: Images obtained from unsplash.com with a creative commons license.

References

Aggarwal, I., & Woolley, A. W. (2019). Team creativity, cognition, and cognitive style diversity. *Management Science*, 65(4), 1586–1599.

Ballerini, M., Cabibbo, N., Candelier, R., Cavagna, A., Cisbani, E., Giardina, I.,... & Zdravkovic, V. (2008). Empirical investigation of starling flocks: A benchmark study in collective animal behaviour. *Animal Behaviour*, 76(1), 201–215.

Bartel, C. A., & Garud, R. (2009). The role of narratives in sustaining organizational innovation. *Organization Science*, 20(1), 107–117.

Bellis, P., & Verganti, R. (2021). Pairs as pivots of innovation: How collaborative sensemaking benefits from innovating in twos. *Innovation*, 23(3), 375–399.

Blei, D. M., Ng, A. Y., & Jordan, M. I. (2003). Latent Dirichlet allocation. *The Journal of Machine Learning Research*, 3, 993–1022.

Blomquist, T., & Lundin, R. A. (2010). Projects – real, virtual or what? *International Journal of Managing Projects in Business*, 3(1), 10–21.

Coghlan, D., Shani, A. B. (Rami), & Dahm, P. (2020). Knowledge production in organization development. *Journal of Change Management*, 20(1), 81–98.

Corley, K. G., & Gioia, D. A. (2004). Identity ambiguity and change in the wake of a corporate spin-off. *Administrative Science Quarterly*, 49(2), 173–208.

Csikszentmihalyi, M., & Getzels, J. W. (1973). The personality of young artists: An empirical and theoretical exploration. *British Journal of Psychology*, 64(1), 91–104.

Cunliffe, A., & Coupland, C. (2012). From hero to villain to hero: Making experience sensible through embodied narrative sensemaking. *Human Relations*, 65(1), 63–88.

De Boom, C., Van Canneyt, S., Demeester, T., & Dhoedt, B. (2016). Representation learning for very short texts using weighted word embedding aggregation. *Pattern Recognition Letters*, 80, 150–156.

Denning, S. (2006). Effective storytelling: Strategic business narrative techniques. *Strategy & Leadership*, 34(1), 42–48.

Dougherty, D., Borrelli, L., Munir, K., & O'Sullivan, A. (2000). Systems of organizational sensemaking for sustained product innovation. *Journal of Engineering and Technology Management*, 17(3–4), 321–355.

Enninga, T., & van der Lugt, R. (2016). The innovation journey and the skipper of the raft: About the role of narratives in innovation project leadership. *Project Management Journal*, 47(2), 103–114.

Farrell, M. P. (2003). *Collaborative circles: Friendship dynamics and creative work*. Chicago, IL: University of Chicago Press.

Frow, P., Nenonen, S., Payne, A., & Storbacka, K. (2015). Managing co-creation design: A strategic approach to innovation. *British Journal of Management*, 26(3), 463–483.

Fulmer, C. A., & Ostroff, C. (2016). Convergence and emergence in organizations: An integrative framework and review. *Journal of Organizational Behavior*, 37, S122–S145.

Garcia Martinez, M. (2015). Solver engagement in knowledge sharing in crowdsourcing communities: Exploring the link to creativity. *Research Policy*, 44(8), 1419–1430.

Green, S. D., & Sergeeva, N. (2019). Value creation in projects: Towards a narrative perspective. *International Journal of Project Management*, 37(5), 636–651.

Harrison, G. W., & List, J. A. (2004). Field experiments. *Journal of Economic Literature*, 42(4), 1009–1055.

Harvey, S. (2014). Creative synthesis: Exploring the process of extraordinary group creativity. *Academy of Management Review*, 39(3), 324–343.

Hill, L. A., Brandeau, G., Truelove, E., & Lineback, K. (2014). *Collective genius: The art and practice of leading innovation*. Boston, MA: Harvard Business Review Press.

Holloway, M. (2009). How tangible is your strategy? how design thinking can turn your strategy into reality. *Journal of Business Strategy*, 30(2–3), 50–56. doi:10.1108/02756660910942463.

Humphreys, M., & Brown, A. D. (2002). Narratives of organizational identity and identification: A case study of hegemony and resistance. *Organization Studies*, 23(3), 421–447.

Hunter, S. T., Cushenbery, L., Fairchild, J., & Boatman, J. (2012). Partnerships in leading for innovation: A dyadic model of collective leadership. *Industrial and Organizational Psychology*, 5(4), 424–428.

Kleiner, A., & Roth, G. (1997). How to make experience your company's best teacher. *Harvard Business Review*, 75(5), 172–178.

Kolko, J. (2010). Abductive thinking and sensemaking: The drivers of design synthesis. *Design Issues*, 26(1), 15–28.
Leonard, D., & Sensiper, S. (1998). The role of tacit knowledge in group innovation. *California Management Review*, 40(3), 112–132.
Maitlis, S., & Christianson, M. (2014). Sensemaking in organizations: Taking stock and moving forward. *Academy of Management Annals*, 8(1), 57–125.
Maitlis, S., & Sonenshein, S. (2010). Sensemaking in crisis and change: Inspiration and insights from Weick (1988). *Journal of Management Studies*, 47 (3), 551–580.
Mikolov, T., Sutskever, I., Chen, K., Corrado, G. S., & Dean, J. (2013). Distributed representations of words and phrases and their compositionality. *Proceedings of the 26th international conference on neural information processing systems - volume 2 (NIPS'13)* (pp. 3111–3119). Curran Associates Inc., Red Hook, NY.
Paulus, P. B., & Nijstad, B. A. (Eds.). (2003). *Group creativity: Innovation through collaboration*. Oxford: Oxford University Press. https://doi.org/10.1093/acprof:oso/9780195147308.001.0001.
Perry-Smith, J. E., & Mannucci, P. V. (2017). From creativity to innovation: The social network drivers of the four phases of the idea journey. *Academy of Management Review*, 42(1), 53–79.
Prager, K. J., & Buhrmester, D. (1998). Intimacy and need fulfillment in couple relationships. *Journal of Social and Personal Relationships*, 15(4), 435–469.
Putman, V. L., & Paulus, P. B. (2009). Brainstorming, brainstorming rules and decision making. *The Journal of Creative Behavior*, 43(1), 29–40.
Reynolds, C. W. (1987). Flocks, herds, and schools: A distributed behavioral model. *Computers and Graphics*, 21, 25–34.
Rhodes, C., & Brown, A. D. (2005). Narrative, organizations and research. *International Journal of Management Reviews*, 7(3), 167–188.
Roloff, M. E., Janiszewski, C. A., McGrath, M. A., Burns, C. S., & Manrai, L. A. (1988). Acquiring resources from intimates when obligation substitutes for persuasion. *Human Communication Research*, 14(3), 364–396.
Rouse, E. D. (2020). Where you end and I begin: Understanding intimate co-creation. *Academy of Management Review*, 45(1), 181–204.
Sandberg, J., & Tsoukas, H. (2015). Making sense of the sensemaking perspective: Its constituents, limitations, and opportunities for further development. *Journal of Organizational Behavior*, 36(S1), S6–S32.
Sanders, E. B. N., & Stappers, P. J. (2008). Co-creation and the new landscapes of design. *Co-design*, 4(1), 5–18.
Shamiyeh, M. (2016). Designing from the future. In Brenner, W., & Uebernickel, F. (Eds.), *Design thinking for innovation* (pp. 193–219). Springer, Cham. https://doi.org/10.1007/978-3-319-26100-3_14.
Stigliani, I., & Ravasi, D. (2012). Organizing thoughts and connecting brains: Material practices and the transition from individual to group-level prospective sensemaking. *Academy of Management Journal*, 55(5), 1232–1259.
Turian, J., Ratinov, L., & Bengio, Y. (2010). Word representations: A simple and general method for semi-supervised learning. *Proceedings of the*

48th annual meeting of the association for computational linguistics (*ACL '10*) (pp. 384–394). Association for Computational Linguistics, USA.

Verganti, R. (2017). *Overcrowded: Designing meaningful products in a world awash with ideas.* Cambridge, MA: MIT Press.

Weick, K. E. (1995). *Sensemaking in organizations (foundations for organizational science).* Thousand Oaks: Sage Publications.

Weick, K. E., Sutcliffe, K. M., & Obstfeld, D. (2005). Organizing and the process of sensemaking. *Organization Science*, 16(4), 409–421.

6 Conclusions

Change is difficult, that is how we started this book. Still, now we know that even if difficult, change can be guided, we can support people to embrace change and transform themselves to make innovation happen. We even know that this can happen with outside-the-box approaches, like asking people to write prospective stories.

Our research focus is on how storymaking affects employees' behaviors in innovation initiatives. Through the action research and design science paradigms, we have sought to also provide relevant insights and methods on how to engage employees in actual transformation projects while utilizing a hybrid research methodology.

This research has revealed many nuances in a design-driven dialog around a story. The four basic elements of the storymaking experience were intentionally designed to explore how to engage people while helping them in their transformation. Specifically, the four basic elements of (1) setting your direction, (2) starting with small, relevant, steps, (3) being critical, and (4) changing with someone else encouraged all participants to leverage what they learned from their transformation projects.

We have observed that active storymaking facilitates the transition from abstract concepts implying change to more operational impacts. These revelations not only encouraged participants to articulate the necessary actions to make change happen, but also offer relevant and unique insights to the innovation literature. Extant research demonstrates the role of stories as a communication tool (Denning, 2006; Bartel & Garud, 2009), and facilitator of sensemaking (Cunliffe & Coupland, 2012). Our collaborative research expands this approach by shifting from linear or one-directional storytelling to circular multidirectional storymaking. The outcome is a much more pragmatic effect resulting from the storymaking process itself, reinforcing the co-creative power of design dialog. In addition to making sense of the new

DOI: 10.4324/9781003276210-6

desired scenario, transformation is enabled through changes in behavior and the requisite actions (Denning, 2006). Our analysis indicates that the new narratives enabled people to revise their cognitive frames, in turn leading to informing action for transformation (Weick, 1995; Blomquist & Lundin, 2010). In particular, the commitments made throughout the episodes helped people gain familiarity with their environment (Enninga & van der Lugt, 2016), and position themselves according to their innovation aspirations. The variety of actions led to multiple reframing (Weick, 1995), shaping new individual and collective identities.

Throughout this storymaking research, we observed the important role that criticism plays in a design dialog intended for transformation. For example, shortly after participants were asked to commit to specific actions, they were then asked to be critical of what they had actually achieved. The literature acknowledges that the adoption of new norms and behaviors might cause discomfort in individuals undertaking change in the organizational context (Kleiner & Roth, 1997). For this reason, critical reflections of the commitments made play a fundamental role in causing individuals to frame uncertainty (Zurlo & Cautela, 2014) and assimilate new external cues to enrich the sensemaking process (Stigliani & Ravasi, 2012). Throughout the sense-perception process, new meanings are continuously shaped and actualized, enabling people to build confidence in overcoming hurdles and inertia to the change they face (Humphreys & Brown, 2002).

Finally, the process of making sense of change through active storymaking is as a compelling way to nurture engagement over time (Martinez, 2015). Throughout the research, the stories became more meaningful as people perceived a deeper sense of clarity in framing and actioning the story. However, the literature acknowledges that telling an engaging story to make innovation happen is still under discussion (Denning, 2006), and our study calls for further investigation of the transformational nature of the meaning-making process, particularly when individuals are the primary actors of the transformation. In fact, shifting from the perspective where stories are employed as a tool to transmit extrinsic business objectives (Denning, 2006; Green & Sergeeva, 2019), narratives can act as a means to guide individuals toward transforming their desired individual and collective identities within their organization (Humphreys & Brown, 2002, Cunliffe & Coupland, 2012).

In summary, our research on how storymaking informs transformation reveals new perspectives on engaging employees in the midst of personal and organizational change. Our intention for the future is to broaden our observations with additional companies and deepen the insights with further data collection.

But there is one more thing that goes back to the opening of this book. We are after all humans before scholars. This book – in our world – represents an innovation. We challenged the status quo, we proposed something new. We left our comfort zone. And we admit it, we were uneasy. We were uneasy because we didn't know how people would react, we knew we were doing things differently from many other workshops and studies over the years and invited partners to collaborate with us in taking a risk in order to derive deeper meaning and understanding of transformation.

We were uneasy the first time we asked a bunch of people to take a piece of paper and start writing their future story of change. We believed it would work. We knew we would guide them there, with all the previous reflections, with all the previous cards. Still, we knew we were taking people outside their comfort zone. We are researchers, we write to live. We write about our studies, but still, we take a blank page and start writing. This is not common for the vast majority of people, and it is definitely not common to write about yourself in a future world. Nevertheless, we did it. And it worked. We have seen people engage, we have seen people ask for more time to finish their stories. We have seen people falling in love with their stories. And this made us happy but still not satisfied. We were satisfied once we saw that happiness became something different. We were satisfied once we saw these people coming back in later weeks with new reflections. Reflections were often not totally aligned with what happened in the first workshop. Still, these were the seeds of new behaviors or at least attempts that had been made in the previous weeks… then becoming something more in the weeks to come. This has nothing to do with burning platforms or grieving, this has to do with people. We have seen happy people write their stories of change and use them as a tool to change and enact new behaviors, the starting point of making innovation happen.

We found our meaning in this innovation, it makes sense for us as human beings because we believe in this collaborative approach. We were engaged in this approach because we co-designed it, we co-built it, card after card. We were satisfied because we built a community around this research, we were influenced and guided by all the people that worked with us in all the organizations. The values we started from are exactly those that we leveraged to build this. We transformed ourselves doing this, and we made a bit of innovation in our researchers world.

This is our wish then: use this book, this collaborative method, as an inspiration to take risks in discovering the meaning of transformation for you, in transforming yourself and your organization such that you can make innovation happen.

References

Bartel, C. A., & Garud, R. (2009). The role of narratives in sustaining organizational innovation. *Organization Science*, 20(1), 107–117.

Blomquist, T., & Lundin, R. A. (2010). Projects–real, virtual or what? *International Journal of Managing Projects in Business*, 3(1), 10–21.

Cunliffe, A., & Coupland, C. (2012). From hero to villain to hero: Making experience sensible through embodied narrative sensemaking. *Human Relations*, 65(1), 63–88.

Denning, S. (2006). Effective storytelling: Strategic business narrative techniques. *Strategy & Leadership*, 34(1), 42–48.

Enninga, T., & van der Lugt, R. (2016). The innovation journey and the skipper of the raft: About the role of narratives in innovation project leadership. *Project Management Journal*, 47(2), 103–114.

Green, S. D., & Sergeeva, N. (2019). Value creation in projects: Towards a narrative perspective. *International Journal of Project Management*, 37(5), 636–651.

Humphreys, M., & Brown, A. D. (2002). Dress and identity: A Turkish case study. *Journal of Management Studies*, 39(7), 927–952.

Kleiner, A., & Roth, G. (1997). How to make experience your company's best teacher. *Harvard Business Review*, 75(5), 172–178.

Martinez, M. G. (2015). Solver engagement in knowledge sharing in crowdsourcing communities: Exploring the link to creativity. *Research Policy*, 44(8), 1419–1430.

Stigliani, I., & Ravasi, D. (2012). Organizing thoughts and connecting brains: Material practices and the transition from individual to group-level prospective sensemaking. *Academy of Management Journal*, 55(5), 1232–1259.

Weick, K. E. (1995). *Sensemaking in organizations* (Vol. 3). Thousand Oaks, CA: Sage Publications.

Zurlo, F., & Cautela, C. (2014). Design strategies in different narrative frames. *Design Issues*, 30(1), 19–35.

What Is IDeaLs?

We live in a constantly changing world where artificial intelligence and digital tools are disrupting our usual way of working and living. Among the most significant challenges for companies to innovate is developing and exploiting the latest technologies and how people engage and make sense of innovation. Embracing innovation requires significant personal effort, since people need to feel a sense of purpose to understand the change and then begin their individual transformation journey.

This is the vision that led to the creation of IDeaLs, the research project that inspired this book. IDeaLs is a research platform pioneering new ways to make innovation happen. Founded by the School of Management of Politecnico di Milano, it aims to unite academics and practitioners in developing relevant insights of the human side of innovation. At IDeaLs, we want to understand how we can engage people to make innovation happen.

In pursuing this objective, IDeaLs brings together leading organizations, thought leaders, and researchers to create actionable tools that spark transformation. In a collaborative research approach, IDeaLs strives to support companies with organizational issues while generating outcomes that are not only relevant to practice but are also scholarly rigorous. IDeaLs works with and within companies seeking to help them tackle specific and concrete innovation challenges using a science-based approach, leveraging methods, tools, and knowledge informed by science. This approach then enables us to develop the tools, methods, and insights that enrich the knowledge of innovation while having a tangible impact on our partner organizations.

Our philosophy is based on three main pillars that guide us as a community in finding new ways to engage people in transformation processes:

DOI: 10.4324/9781003276210-7

1 ***Innovation as meaning***. We strongly believe that people are motivated by a personal sense of purpose. This means that in any change or transformation situation, each individual needs to find meaning, and the reason to join the quest. Therefore, we believe that nurturing people's engagement in organizational transformation means supporting them in finding their sense of purpose.

2 ***Design as engagement***. We believe that people engage when they can visualize the intentions and co-create the artifact. Studies show that in any activity (e.g., solving a problem, assembling a new product), people's emotional attachment to the activity and its outcome increases if they are able to directly touch it, both cognitively and physically. Therefore, we leverage design tools and practices to enable organizational actors to shape, live, and feel the transformation directly in the first person.

3 ***Leadership as community***. We believe that people engage when they are not alone in the transformation. An organization is an ecosystem of a multitude of people; it can change if all its actors change smoothly. Therefore, people need to perceive they are part of a community taking collective action toward change.

IDeaLs officially kicked off in September 2018 with the first community meeting. The first edition was made possible thanks to the collaboration with our partner organizations: Adobe, Adidas, Centre for Creative Leadership, Nestlé, Philips, Sintetica, Sorgenia, and Stolt Tankers. However, this volume is based on the experiences with our partners in the second edition (the protagonists in Chapter 4), also welcoming on board Sasol and STEF. Over the past three years, IDeaLs has collaborated with many international organizations that stand together in their belief that innovation is not only about an output, it is about people.

By engaging more than 1,000 people from the various IDeaLs partner organizations, we have discovered how to engage people in innovation by creating a sense of ownership before asking them to take action toward a transformative direction.

This volume is one of the tangible outcomes of the research we developed together, and we thank each and every one for their invaluable contributions.

Index

Note: **Bold** page numbers refer to tables and *italic* page numbers refer to figures.

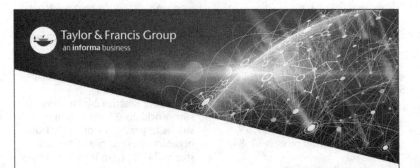

Printed in the United States
by Baker & Taylor Publisher Services